Essential Ear Training
for Today's Musician

Steve Prosser

Berklee Media

Vice President: Dave Kusek
Dean of Continuing Education: Debbie Cavalier
Business Manager: Rob Green
Technology Manager: Mike Serio
Marketing Manager, Berkleemusic: Barry Kelly
Senior Designer: David Ehlers

Berklee Press

Sr. Writer/Editor: Jonathan Feist
Writer/Editor: Susan Gedutis
Production Manager: Shawn Girsberger Marketing
Manager, Berklee Press: Jennifer Rassler Product
Marketing Manager: David Goldberg

ISBN: 978-0-634-00640-1

Berklee
Press

1140 Boylston Street
Boston, MA 02215-3693 USA
(617) 747-2146

Visit Berklee Press Online at
www.berkleepress.com

DISTRIBUTED BY

HAL•LEONARD®
7777 W. BLUEMOUND RD. P.O. BOX 13819
MILWAUKEE, WISCONSIN 53213

Visit Hal Leonard Online
www.halleonard.com

DEDICATION

This modest textbook is dedicated, with deepest love and respect, to my late parents—Bill Prosser, who survived the brutal chaos of Omaha Beach, and Betty Prosser, who dressed wounds and soothed the wounded from the Battle of the Bulge—and to all Depression-era veterans whose sacrifices endowed my generation with the freedom and leisure to pursue learning and artistic expression.

FOREWORD

Berklee College of Music is known and respected for many things; the Ear Training Department is certainly one of them. Now, for the first time, students who want to learn ear training the Berklee way can do so with *Essential Ear Training*.

Author and Chair of the Ear Training Department, Steve Prosser, has combined his musicianship and twenty years of teaching experience to create this comprehensive collection. This book will take you as far as you're willing to go. The material starts with basic diatonic exercises in common time, and moves on to studies that utilize both mixed meter and mixed modality.

Essential Ear Training assumes a basic understanding of music theory. Students using this book should be able to:

- read notes in treble and bass clef,
- recognize all key signatures,
- read a variety of rhythms and time signatures, and
- recognize all major and minor scales and modes.

Steve Prosser addresses many learning styles throughout the exercises by isolating or removing different musical elements. Workshop activities include:

Rhythmic Studies which focus on rhythm, freeing the student from solfège and key signatures.

Sight Recognition Studies focusing on solfège, removing the element of rhythm.

Sol-fa Studies which focus on solfège functions without the added difficulty of note reading.

Melodic Studies containing examples similar to those found in a musician's daily work.

Practicing the Lessons and Workshops in this collection will bring your ear-training chops to the next level!

Debbie Cavalier
Managing Editor
Berklee Press

CONTENTS

PREFACE

Ear training is among the most important skills to be studied by the music student. The goal of ear-training study is to help musicians master the basic components of musical craft: to assist music readers in hearing the music they are seeing; to aid writers in notating music they have composed or arranged; to help performers in developing their musical vocabulary; and to assist listeners in understanding the music they are hearing. Ear training helps the performer learn his part. It helps the composer write when she is away from her instrument. It helps the conductor to study his score. It helps all musicians whenever they discuss music. It develops the inner ear and provides the creative imagination with a musical lexicon.

Essential Ear Training is divided into two parts. Part One includes Lessons that discuss ear training concepts and suggest a means of practice for each ear training topic—this is particularly useful for students studying on their own. Part Two reinforces these concepts with practice exercises called Workshops that will provide the student with a well-balanced foundation in ear training.

The Lessons are in the following order of topics:

Lesson 1: Conducting Patterns (when a new pattern is first introduced)
Lesson 2: Rhythmic Studies
Lesson 3: Sight Recognition Studies
Lesson 4: Sol-fa Studies
Lesson 5: Melodic Studies
Lesson 6: Supplemental Lesson: Visualization-Improvisation

You may wish to read through all of the Lessons before undertaking the Workshops, or you may prefer to jump right into the first Workshop. Refer back to the Lessons in Part One as needed.

If this book is used in a classroom, instructors are encouraged to use material from the Workshops to supplement and support other ideas or techniques they may have developed themselves.

Essential Ear Training is the result of three decades of performing, writing, and teaching music. Students who study and master the concepts and exercises in this book will provide themselves with a solid musical foundation for whatever musical career they pursue.

Steve Prosser
Boston
January, 2000

PART ONE—LESSONS

LESSON ONE: CONDUCTING PATTERNS

It is strongly recommended that conducting patterns be used for all Workshops in this book (where time signatures are used). The primary purpose of using conducting patterns is to provide you with a tool to keep time (by virtue of the beats) and to supply spatial awareness (by virtue of the position of the beats). Some ear training methods suggest that students tap their hands or feet while singing. Tapping is good for time keeping but not for telling you where you are in the bar of music you are reading. A conducting pattern effectively accomplishes both of these tasks.

The most common time signature is 4/4. Here is the standard conducting pattern for 4/4 time:

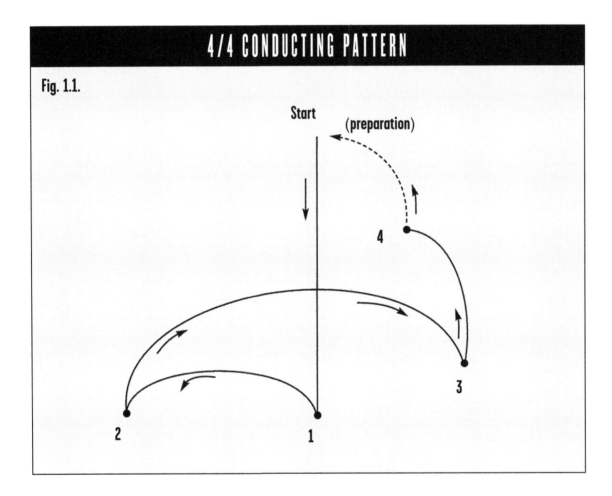

Move your hand according to these directions: Down, left, right, up. One, two, three, four. Down, left, right, up.

This is how the 4/4 conducting pattern relates to music notation:

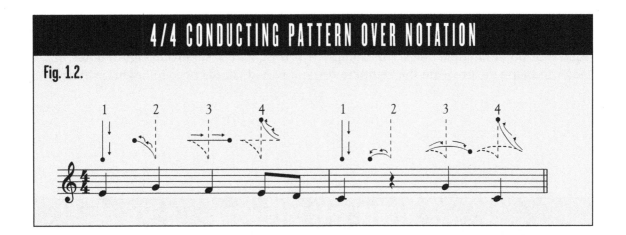

Practice the 4/4 pattern until you can do it without thinking too much about it. Style is not as important as a well-defined beat pattern. Once you are comfortable conducting, you can integrate it into your ear training exercises. This integration may be difficult at first, but with regular practice, the separate tasks of conducting and singing will fit together naturally. New conducting patterns will be introduced throughout this book. Get comfortable with each new pattern before you begin integrating conducting and singing.

Lesson One
CONDUCTING PATTERNS

Subdivisions

When reading certain rhythms, it can be helpful to subdivide a beat.

You can vary your conducting pattern to articulate beat subdivisions by simply hitting each beat point multiple times. For example, if you wanted to subdivide eighth notes, in order to help you articulate the eighth notes, you would conduct the following pattern:

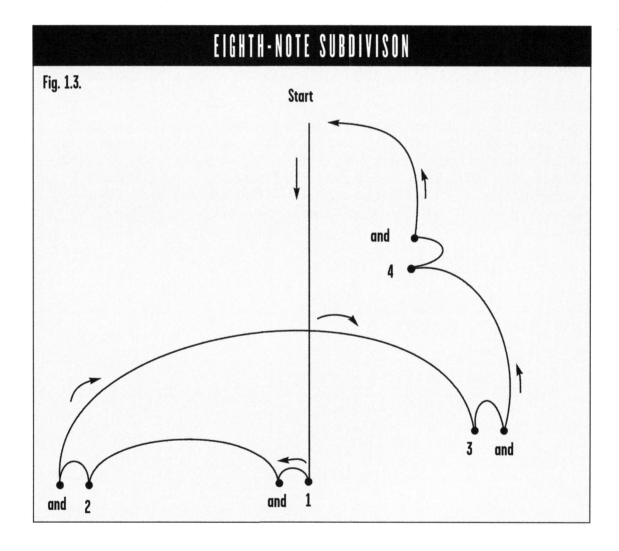

EIGHTH-NOTE SUBDIVISON

Fig. 1.3.

Start

and

4

3   and

and   2

and   1

You can also use the eighth-note conducting subdivision to help you sing sixteenth notes. While conducting the eighth-note subdivision, you should count to yourself, "One ee and ah, two ee and ah, three ee and ah, four ee and ah." This subdivision should be used on rhythms that include sixteenth notes.

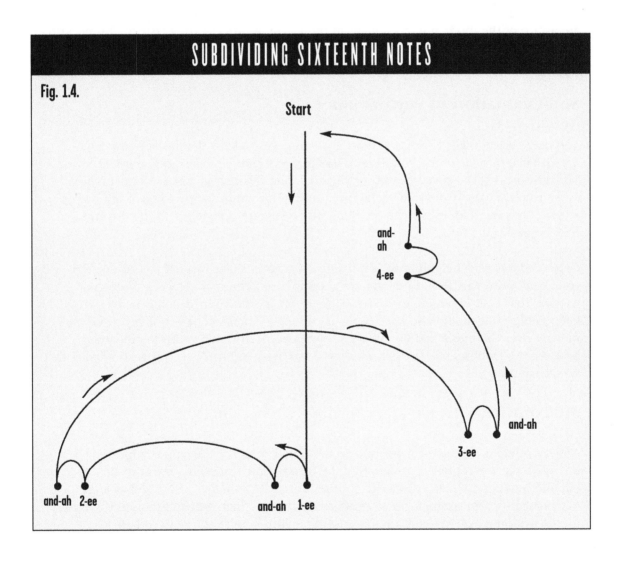

SUBDIVIDING SIXTEENTH NOTES

Fig. 1.4.

LESSON TWO: RHYTHMIC STUDIES

An effective strategy for sight reading music is to break it down into simpler, more manageable tasks and mastering those first. Practicing rhythm removed from pitches is an example.

Performance and Tempo

The rhythmic exercises should be performed while conducting. You will find that "tuh" and "tut" (for long and short durations) or similar syllables are suitable for rhythmic singing. The tempo of each exercise should be determined by you. The best tempo is the one that allows you to concentrate on three important characteristics of good performance—a steady beat, accurate articulations, and correct note durations.

Balancing all of those considerations at once suggests that you start with a slow tempo. Don't interpret a slow tempo as a sign of inability—just the opposite—it shows that you are aware of the more important goals in the learning process: the mastery of time, articulation, and duration. As you gain confidence in the performance of each new set of rhythms, tempo may be raised to whatever challenge you desire.

Self-Evaluation of Performance

You may ask yourself, "How do I know if my time is solid, my durations correct, or my articulations accurate?" You have to take responsibility for this and, simply put, self-awareness is the answer, whether you are using this text in a classroom situation or by yourself. Again, this consideration touches on tempo. Go slowly enough so you know *how* you are doing *as* you are doing it—if you are not sure, slow down—it is that simple!

Conducting is very helpful in self-evaluation of your performance. If you notice that your hand is beating beat 4 but you are reading beat 2, there is clearly a problem. Assume that your conducting hand is correct. Try to find your place in the music and keep going. You should also keep going if you make a mistake. Try to keep your eye moving over the music and jump back in when you can. Then go back and slowly practice the troublesome rhythm until you have mastered it. Then go back and sing the whole rhythm.

Metronomes

A metronome is useful in ear training. In the initial stages of learning rhythms or melodies, the metronome, by mirroring the beats of the time signature and the conducting pattern, helps you to keep time. The metronome is also useful as a tool of articulation. For example, in an exercise in 4/4 time that uses eighth-note rhythms, the metronome may be set at the pace of the eighth-note subdivision to help you with articulation.

EIGHTH-NOTE SUBDIVISONS IN 4/4 TIME

Fig. 2.1.

In the example above, the metronome should be set to the eighth-note subdivision. While conducting, sing the example slowly, paying careful attention to the relationship between your articulations and the beats of the metronome. Use of the metronome in more difficult rhythms (such as highly syncopated rhythms) helps provide an ensemble context of time and counterpoint, which helps build rhythmic independence. If you are active in music technology, you may want to substitute a drum machine or sequencer/MIDI device combination for the metronome. The potential for creating a greater ensemble context with the use of these types of instruments is great.

A final note on use of the metronome: As useful a tool as it is, the metronome limits its user—it doesn't allow for variation of feel and tempo. Additionally, you must establish a reliable inner clock of your own. This comes only after much practice and musical experience, but it is a skill that must be learned. Thus, you are advised to practice with and without the metronome—with it during the initial stages of working on rhythmic problems or when an ensemble context is desired, and without it as mastery of rhythms is gained and the sense of the internal clock is strengthened.

Duets

In addition to being able to keep time and to perform rhythms accurately, it is essential that you be able to coordinate your rhythmic sense with that of other musicians. The duets allow you to do rhythms in tag-team style. Two individual students start, one on each part. As they proceed through the duet, the class leader cues other students to jump in and take over one part or the other.

If you are studying these duets alone, use a tape recorder. Start your recorder, count off a few beats and then sing one of the parts. Then sing the duet along with the recording. Repeat this procedure for the other part.

Ideally, you should practice duet exercises with another student. If these exercises are used in a classroom situation, students can be divided into two groups, one on each part.

LESSON THREE: SIGHT RECOGNITION (PITCH) STUDIES

At Berklee, I have found that movable-do solfège, as opposed to fixed-do solfège, is the most successful ear training method for contemporary musicians. In fixed-do solfège, the note C is always Do, D is Re, and so on; in movable-do solfège, the one or tonic of the key is Do. Fixed-Do solfège teaches you to hear intervallic relationships. Moveable-Do solfège teaches you to hear functional relationships related to particular solfège syllables. Hearing functional relationships allows you to understand the general structure of melody when you hear it (whether you know the key or not), allows you to transpose easily to other keys, and helps you to hear harmonies as well. The use of movable-do requires you to learn the relationships of the notes of every key and the corresponding solfège syllables. That seems like a large task, but understanding the melodic functions of each key is very useful for a musician, and the many advantages of movable-do solfège mastery clearly outweigh that difficulty.

The Solfège Syllables

Solfège syllables are based on the diatonic major scale. Here they are in the key of C major:

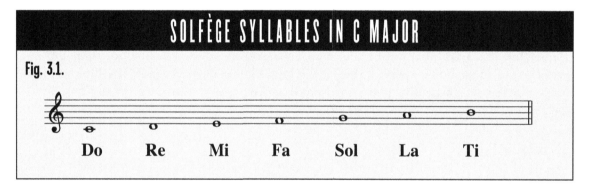

These syllables are often called solfège functions to reinforce that they are actually expressing relationships and functionality rather than specific pitches. Here are the major solfège syllables in the key of G major:

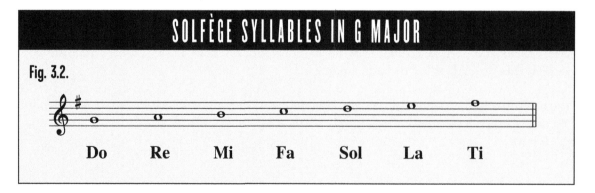

As you can see, the syllables are the same.

Chromatic alterations of these notes are indicated with altered vowel endings of the syllables. Sharped notes are indicated with syllables using the vowel alteration "i" (pronounced like a long "e," as in the "i" in "diva").

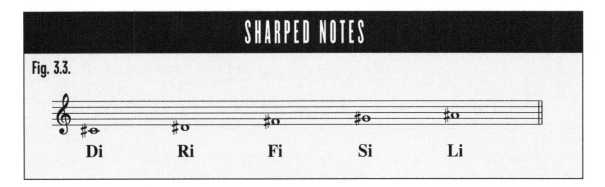

Flatted notes are indicated with syllables ending in the vowel alteration "a" (like the "a" in "father") or "e" (like the "e" in "grey").

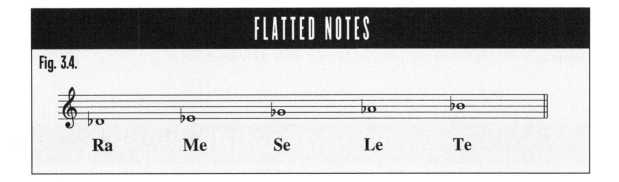

This means that the same pitch will be sung with a different syllable depending on how it functions. The two notes indicated below are enharmonically equivalent but functionally different and, therefore, have different syllables. Di's functional tendency is to resolve upward. Ra's tendency is to resolve downward.

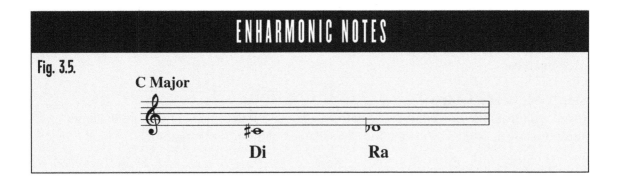

Lesson Three
SIGHT RECOGNITION (PITCH) STUDIES

Here, then, is the chromatic set of all solfège syllables, presented in the key of C major:

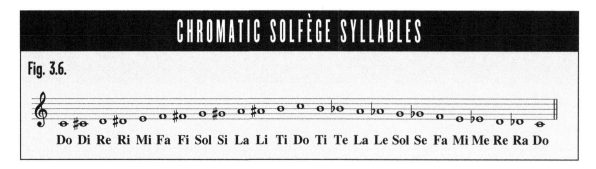

CHROMATIC SOLFÈGE SYLLABLES

Fig. 3.6.

Do Di Re Ri Mi Fa Fi Sol Si La Li Ti Do Ti Te La Le Sol Se Fa Mi Me Re Ra Do

With practice, these syllables are easily integrated with your sense of pitch functions, and they are a great aid in the reading and comprehension of music.

Sight Recognition

Sight recognition studies help you associate solfège functions with notes. This technique is taught in isolation from other aspects of ear training; the studies have no rhythm and no time signature—just note heads.

Practice the sight recognition studies in this book by saying the syllable for each note, keeping steady time. (Metronomes are helpful with these exercises.)

Here is an example of a sight recognition study:

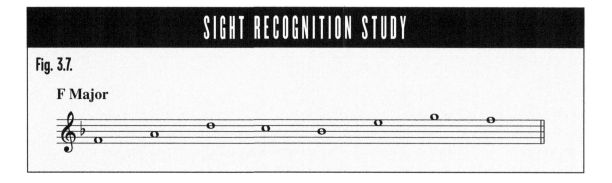

SIGHT RECOGNITION STUDY

Fig. 3.7.

F Major

Step One: Find "Do"
In this example, we are in the key of F, so F is Do. Silently scan the staff, quickly orienting yourself to the solfège syllable for each note. The scale is indicated in each exercise.

Step Two: Beat a tempo
Using a metronome or a conducting pattern, choose a tempo fast enough to challenge you but slow enough so you can find the syllables without breaking time.

Step Three: Say each syllable in time
In this example, you would say, "Do Mi La Sol Fa Ti Re Do." If you miss a beat, slow down the tempo or alternate saying notes and resting on every other beat. If you can do this exercise easily, speed up the tempo. Practice each sight recognition study until you can perform it comfortably at a fast tempo.

LESSON FOUR: SOL-FA STUDIES

Hearing and singing sol-fa is a process of deriving musical pitches from reading solfège functions (Do, Re, Mi, and so on) without the added difficulty of reading specific notes. Sol-fa is an effective way to introduce music reading because it generalizes the melodic functions of tonal music before you have to relate them to a particular key. This is an aspect of movable-do solfège which is most advantageous for the contemporary musician. The ability to generally understand the function and form of sound (the hearing part) not only provides you with a useful musical ability, it also prepares you to relate general sound to specific notes (the seeing part). Thus, if you can hear a melody (by sol-fa function) in the key of C, you will also be able to hear it in the key of F♯. The sol-fa exercises in this book are based on an assumption that you can sing a major scale and that you can apply the appropriate solfège syllables to that scale. A typical sol-fa study looks like this:

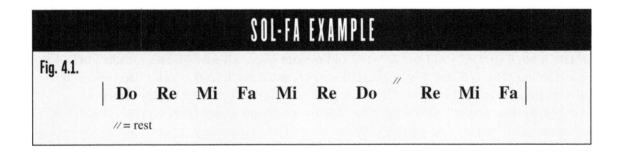

How to Do the Sol-fa Studies

In addition to your metronome, you will need a device to give you your starting pitch. This can be a pitch wheel, a tuning fork, or just your instrument. Using a piano is fine, but it should be used only for the starting pitch and for checking the final pitch on a given exercise. Avoid playing melodies on the piano before or after singing. In studying the exercises in this book, you will try to form sounds and build a memory of functional relationships—not match pitches.

Step One: Choose "Do"
Play a note on your pitch source; any pitch will do. It is a good idea to start exercises on a variety of starting pitches rather than the same one every time. Your starting pitch will be "Do," the tonic of the key of your exercise; it may or may not be the first note of the exercise.

Step Two: Sing the first syllable
If "Do" is the first syllable of the exercise, this will be easy since you already hear it in your mind. If the first syllable is not "Do," you will need to find it. You can do this by singing up or down the scale from "Do."

Step Three: Find the next note
Imagine (hear) and then sing the next syllable. Notice that when you imagine the pitch, your throat moves into position to sing. This part of the exercise is called inner hearing and is very important in developing your ear. So, it is very important to use the silence between pitches to develop a vivid inner sound.

Lesson Four

SOL-FA STUDIES

Step Four: Verify your pitch

Once you complete the exercise, sing "Do" or your last pitch, and check it against your pitch source. If it is not in tune, it means that you either missed one of the pitches or your intonation was inaccurate. You must try to go slowly enough to avoid mistakes and to keep your intonation true. Remember that accuracy—not speed—is your goal!

Hearing Solfège Functions

In movable-do solfège, "Do" is always the tonic (the point of rest). All of the other notes have an implied resolution to "Do." That implied resolution is the key to learning the solfège functions.

It is easy to hear solfège functions that are close together, such as "Do" to "Re" in the example above. But what if the note after Re was "La?" The best way to find "La" is to relate it back to "Do"—not to "Re." The old maxim goes, "All roads lead to Rome." In ear training, "Do" is Rome. If you hear all notes relating back to the tonic "Do," you will always be able to find your way. You will not only sing an accurate solfège function every time, but you will also develop a reliable long-term memory of each sol-fa function.

Octaves

At each new syllable, you must choose the octave in which to place it. Generally, it is easiest to choose the octave approached by the smaller interval. If you see "Sol Ti," you would usually choose to go up a major third rather than down a minor sixth. However, you may choose otherwise if the line is pushing the limits of your vocal range or if you wish to practice larger leaps.

LESSON FIVE: MELODIC STUDIES

Melodic studies integrate all other studies in this book—conducting, rhythm, and solfège. These studies present exercises that are just like musical examples you will see in your daily work as a musician. You will find that solfège is an important tool when you look at or discuss any music, and these exercises will be good practice.

Here is an example of a melodic study:

How to Do Melodic Studies

Step One: Say the solfège of the melody
Before doing the rhythms or pitches, say the solfège syllables on a constant pulse. Use the metronome to help you keep the beat. This will identify any sight recognition problems.

Step Two: Say the solfège with the rhythm
Set the metronome at a slow tempo. Say the solfège with the rhythm and conduct—concentrate on your articulation and durations. Go slowly enough so you know you are saying the right rhythms. If you find a particular rhythm that is very difficult, isolate that rhythm and practice it; then say the whole example again. This step isolates rhythmic difficulties.

Step Three: Sing the solfège alone
Give yourself a G on your pitch instrument. Without tempo or rhythm, sing (using solfège) the first note of the example. Hold the note as long as it takes to establish a good pitch. You have to decide what that is, so take your time. Stop. Look at the next note and try to get the sound of the solfège into your head. When you have heard the pitch, sing it; again hold the note until you are satisfied with the intonation. Finish the example in the same way. This helps you identify solfège relationships (jumps or chromatic notes usually) that are problematic.

Lesson Five

MELODIC STUDIES

Step Four: Sing the example

By now you should have discovered potential problems in the singing of the example. Set a slow tempo and, while conducting, begin singing. It is important that you sing through the example—don't stop. If you get lost, try to find your place or try to find Do. If the tempo was too fast, reset the metronome to a slower tempo and start the example again. If you find that there is still a particular problem in sight recognition, rhythm, or solfège, isolate the problem and practice it before you try singing the whole example again.

Some melodic examples will not require going through all of these steps. Some examples will present rhythmic problems, so you would have to practice only Step Two. Another example might pose a particularly difficult melodic section. You would apply Step Three to master the problem. Eventually, as your sight recognition, rhythms, and solfège improve you will gradually be able to move away from the step system altogether.

Duets

Each chapter concludes with a melodic duet. As with the duets in the Rhythmic Studies, they may be practiced by groups or alone. See Lesson Two for more tips on practicing duets.

LESSON SIX: SUPPLEMENTAL LESSON: VISUALIZATION-IMPROVISATION

Visualization-improvisation is a supplemental exercise to complement your sol-fa and melodic studies. The goal of visualization-improvisation, as the name suggests, is to see in your mind pitches on a musical instrument as you sing melodies of your own creation. The preferred instrument for this exercise is a piano because of its common use in all aspects of music, but your instrument (guitar frets or sax fingerings), or even an image of musical notation, can be used.

The results of extensive practice in visualization-improvisation are profound. One of the primary goals of any musician should be to make the musical mind a competent, secure, and flexible instrument in and of itself. The ability of that musical mind to internally create or interpret external musical sound is a result of accomplishing that goal. That ability has important ramifications for musical use: the skill to envision music as it is composed, leaving only a final task of physical notation; the capacity to see printed music and to hear that music without playing it on an instrument; and the proficiency to hear played or recorded music and to understand its shape and form, possibly to the extent of seeing in the mind's eye the notes as they are played and heard. These are, most certainly, worthwhile abilities to seek through study. And note that these abilities are both analogous and complementary to the act of sight reading. Most important, though, these are abilities that can be learned through visualization-improvisation when combined with the other studies in this ear training book.

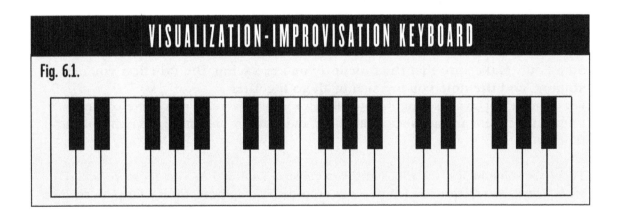

VISUALIZATION-IMPROVISATION KEYBOARD

Fig. 6.1.

The keyboard in Figure 6.1. is for demonstrating the visualization-improvisation technique. Look at the keyboard and then close your eyes. Try to see the keyboard. Run up and down the chromatic notes from C up to a higher C. If you can visualize all the notes as you go, then you are ready to proceed with the exercises. If you decide to use another visualization device, try the same experiment with your eyes closed. If you are using guitar or bass frets, try moving up through a chromatic scale starting on one of your strings. No matter which instrument you choose to see, you have to decide if your sense of the structure of the instrument as your mind sees it is vivid enough to add the difficulties of function and pitch. If you cannot yet visualize any instrument, then you should use the keyboard provided in conjunction with your exercises. When you feel more confident about the structure of the keyboard, you can experiment with your eyes closed.

When should you start trying the exercises? The best answer is that you should start when you begin to feel confident with a certain component of your studies. For instance, in the early workshops of the book, you deal with major key melodies in the sol-fa studies. When you start to feel confident about the sounds and related functions of the major scale, you should begin to practice visualization-improvisation.

Lesson Six
SUPPLEMENTAL LESSON: VISUALIZATION-IMPROVISATION

Visualization-Improvisation Example

The best way to begin with visualization-improvisation is to try singing without a tempo—just to feel your way around the keyboard. For this introductory exercise, just give yourself a starting pitch of C. For this example, let's use the major scale in the key of C. Close your eyes and see the note and sing it, saying the sol-fa function Do. Once you are satisfied with your pitch, stop. Then, with your eyes closed, see the next ascending note, D. Get the pitch in your head, and when you are sure of the pitch, sing it as Re, then stop. Continue in this fashion up and down the scale. Then you can try improvising stepwise motion of your own choice (such as Do Re Mi Re Mi Fa Sol La Sol Fa Mi Fa Mi Re Do, and so on). Once you are secure with the basic sight and sound of the scale, then you can add the difficulty of time and rhythm. Use the following technique:

Step One: Start with a very slow pulse on the metronome
Again, setting the tempo is most important. Don't hesitate to go very slowly at first.

Step Two: Give yourself a reference pitch and visualize it
Give yourself the Do of the key.

Step Three: Sing the pitch and start creating a melody, singing on one beat and resting on the next: sing – pause – sing
Use whatever component you are working on in a given chapter. If you are working on stepwise melodies in sol-fa, do them in visualization-improvisation.

Step Four: Make sure that the function you are saying, the function you are singing, and the note you are seeing all go together
For example, if you are seeing the note B in a C major exercise, make sure you are singing the note B and not some other note, and that you are saying the right solfège function, Ti.

There are some logical variations of the exercise as outlined. As you get more secure with visualization-improvisation, you can drop the resting beats from your performance or you can improvise in a rhythmic context over the metronome pulse. You may also want to practice visualization-improvisation without any metronome pulse and work toward more freely phrased melodies. You might want to work on visualization of the staff, using treble and bass clefs, working through the various keys and intervals. These latter types of exercises suggest one of the practical uses of melodic visualization discussed earlier—the ability to see as you compose. Indeed, it is hoped that you will find visualization-improvisation the most ultimately practical and aesthetically meaningful musical exercises you will undertake in the study of this book.

This is an activity you can take with you as you walk down the street, drive your car, or sit quietly in a room. And it is an activity that will help prepare you for the working tasks of music: composition, improvisation, reading and understanding music. Thus, although you will not see specific exercises or references to visualization-improvisation in the Workshop section of this book, you are strongly encouraged to make it a part of your daily musical work. You will find it well worth the added work.

PART TWO—WORKSHOPS

Workshop One

RHYTHMIC STUDIES

Practice the following rhythmic studies using the syllables "tuh" and "tut." Remember to conduct in 4/4 while performing these examples. For additional help, see the rhythmic studies lesson on page 8.

Practice the following duets with another student, or use a tape recorder. See page 13
for ideas about practicing alone.

DUETS

9

10

Workshop One

SIGHT RECOGNITION STUDIES

Sight recognition studies help you focus on solfège functions without rhythms or time signatures. See page 16 for additional information about sight recognition studies.

The following sight recognition exercises are in the major keys of C, G, F, and B♭.

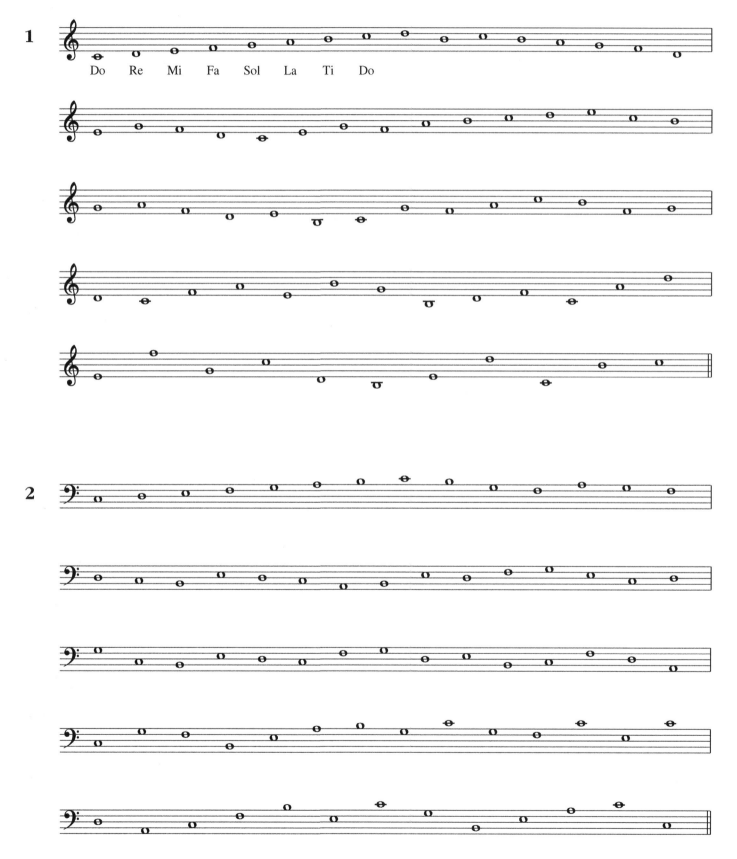

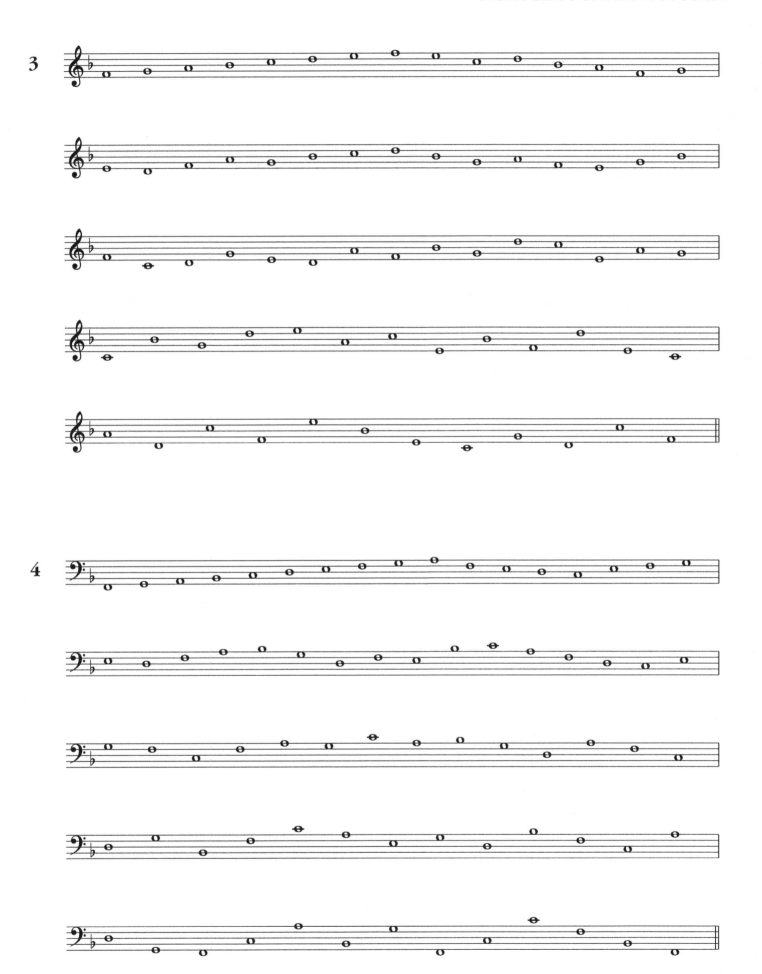

Workshop One
SIGHT RECOGNITION STUDIES

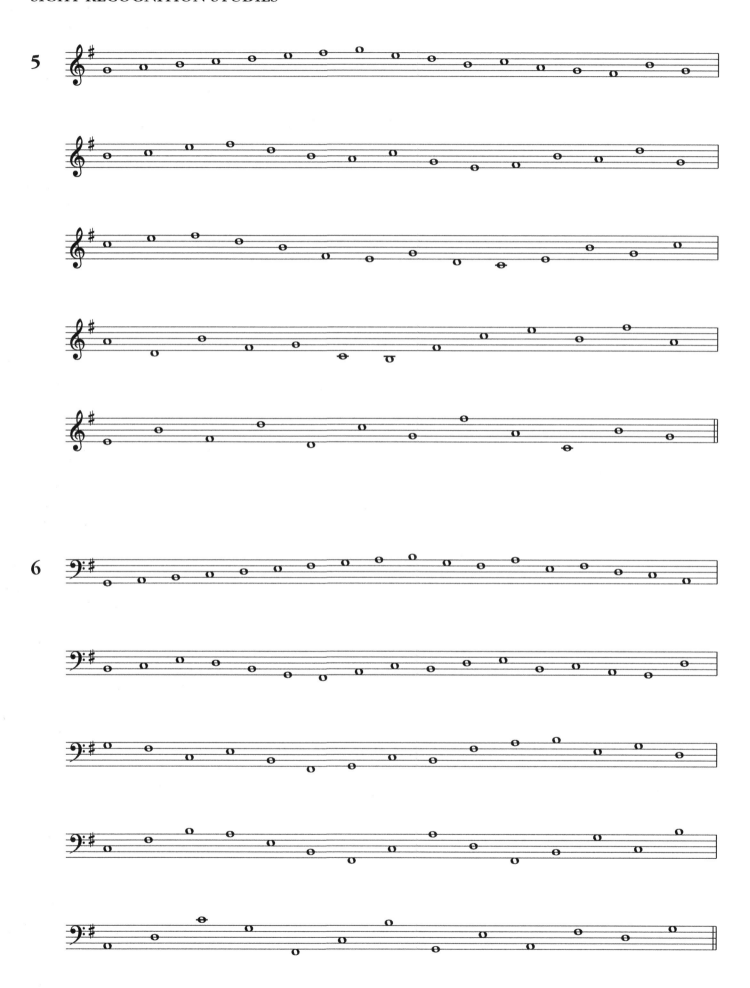

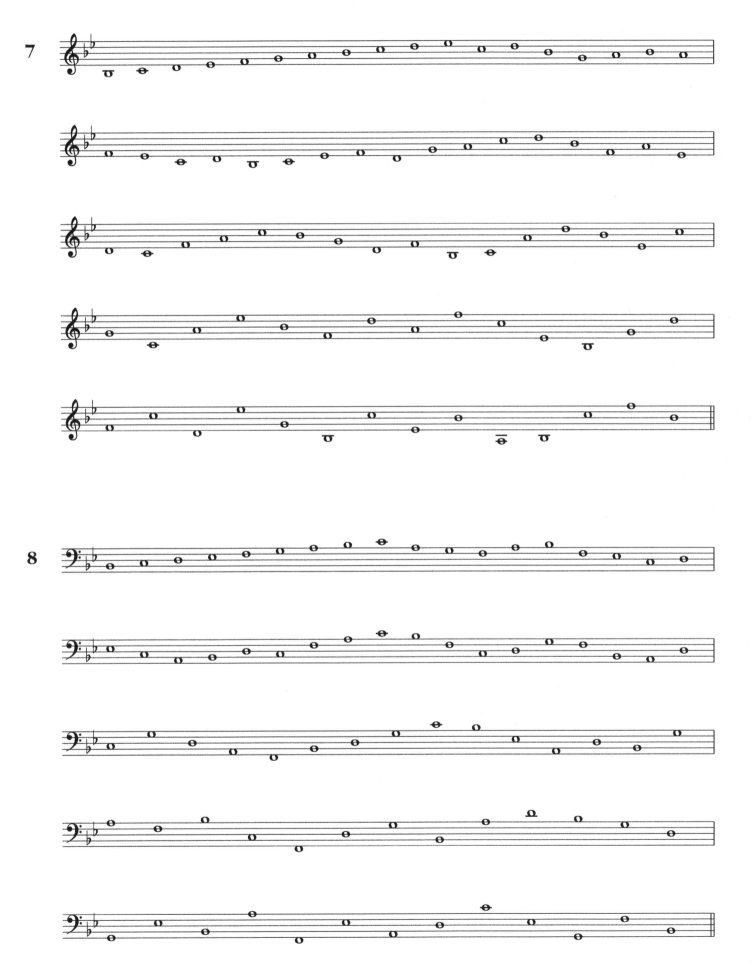

Workshop One

SOL-FA STUDIES

The sol-fa studies will help you with the melodic functions of tonal music without relating them to a particular key. See page 17 for a step-by-step approach to sol-fa studies. The following sol-fa exercises focus on small melodic motions.

// = rest and take a breath.

1 Do Re Mi Fa Mi Re Do //   Re Mi Fa Sol La Ti Do //

   Do Ti La Sol La Sol Fa //   Mi Re Do Ti Do Re Do

2 Do Mi Re Do Mi Fa Sol //   La Fa Sol Fa Mi Do Re //

   Do Mi Re Mi Fa Sol La //   Ti La Sol Fa Mi Re Do //

3 Do La Sol La Do Re Do //   La Do Re Fa Mi Do Re //

   Do La Do Re Mi Sol Fa //   Sol La Ti Re Mi Re Do La Do

MELODIC STUDIES

Melodic studies combine the skills used in the rhythmic, sol-fa, and sight recognition studies. See page 19 for more information about doing melodic studies.

Conduct and sing the following in stepwise melodies in the keys of C, G, F, and B♭ major.

Workshop One

MELODIC STUDIES

Practice the following duets with another student, or use a tape recorder. See page 20
for some ideas about practicing alone.

MELODIC DUETS

18

19

Workshop Two

CONDUCTING PATTERNS

There are two new conducting patterns in Workshop Two. See Lesson One for a discussion of conducting pattern practice

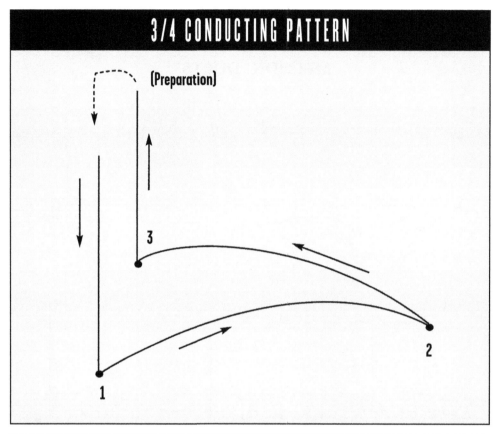

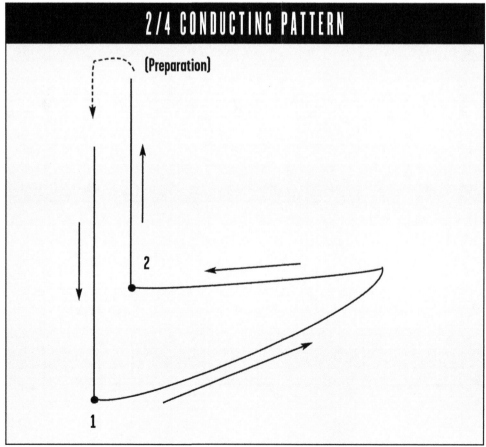

Practice the following rhythmic studies in 3/4 and 2/4 time signatures. Some of the exercises in this workshop use tied rhythms. Remember to conduct while performing the examples.

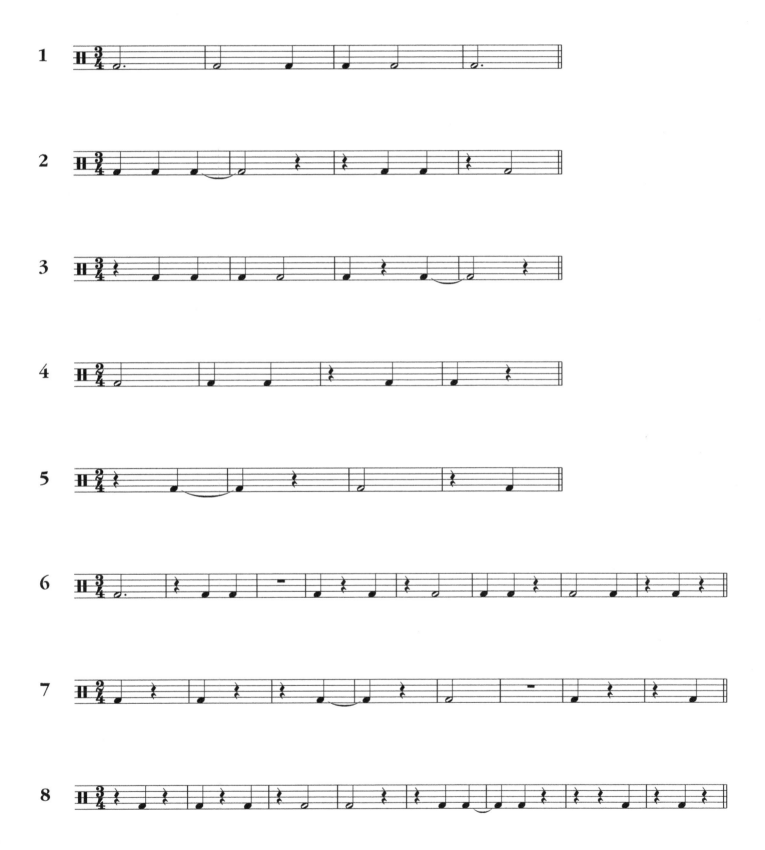

Workshop Two

RHYTHMIC STUDIES

DUETS

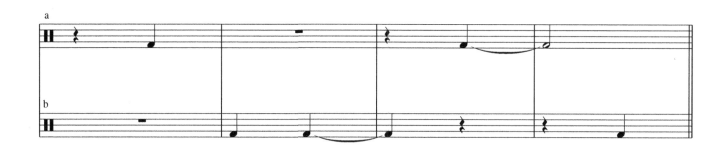

The following sight recognition exercises are in the keys of D, E♭, A, and A♭ major.

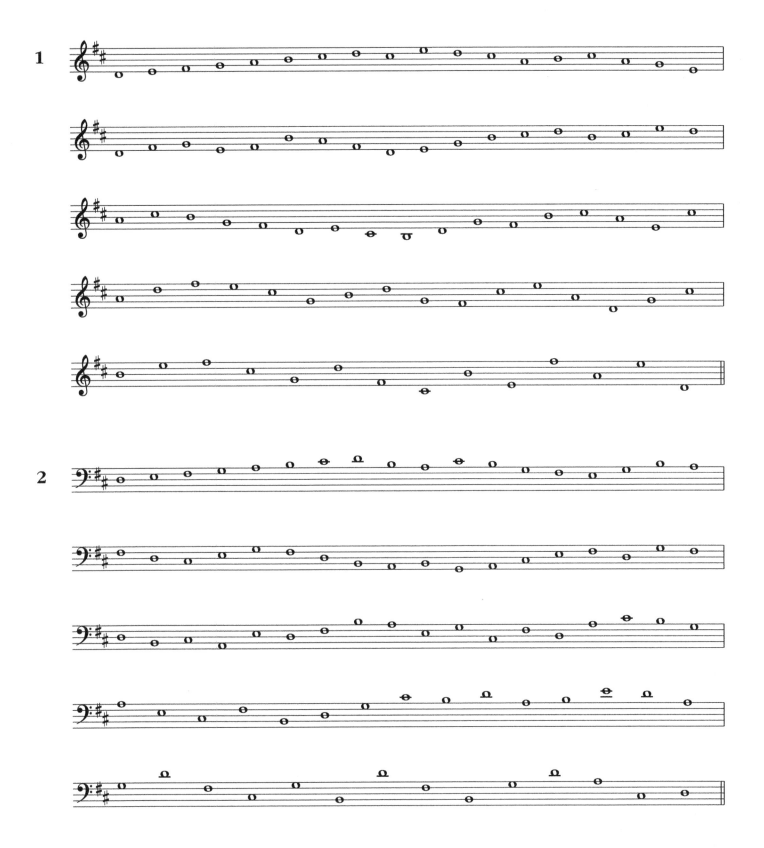

Workshop Two

SIGHT RECOGNITION STUDIES

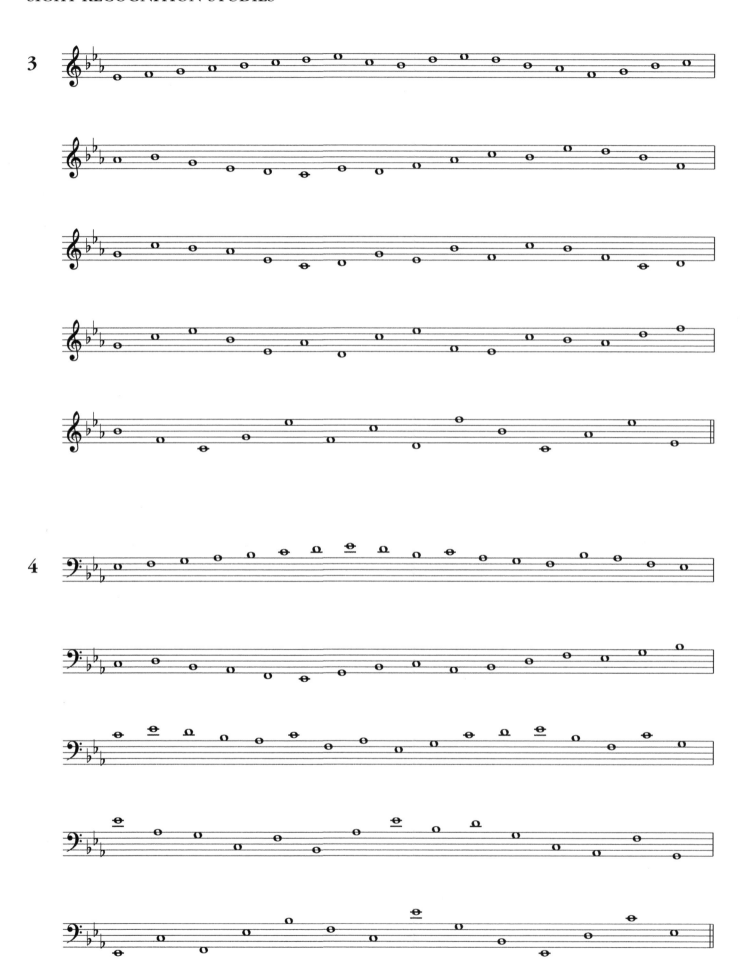

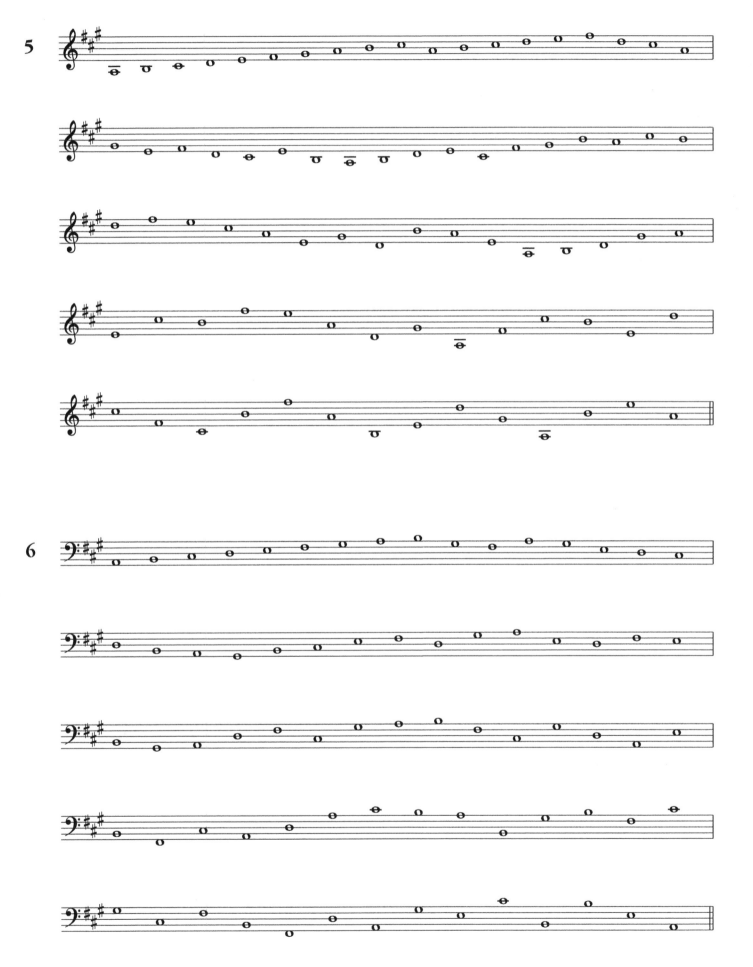

Workshop Two
SIGHT RECOGNITION STUDIES

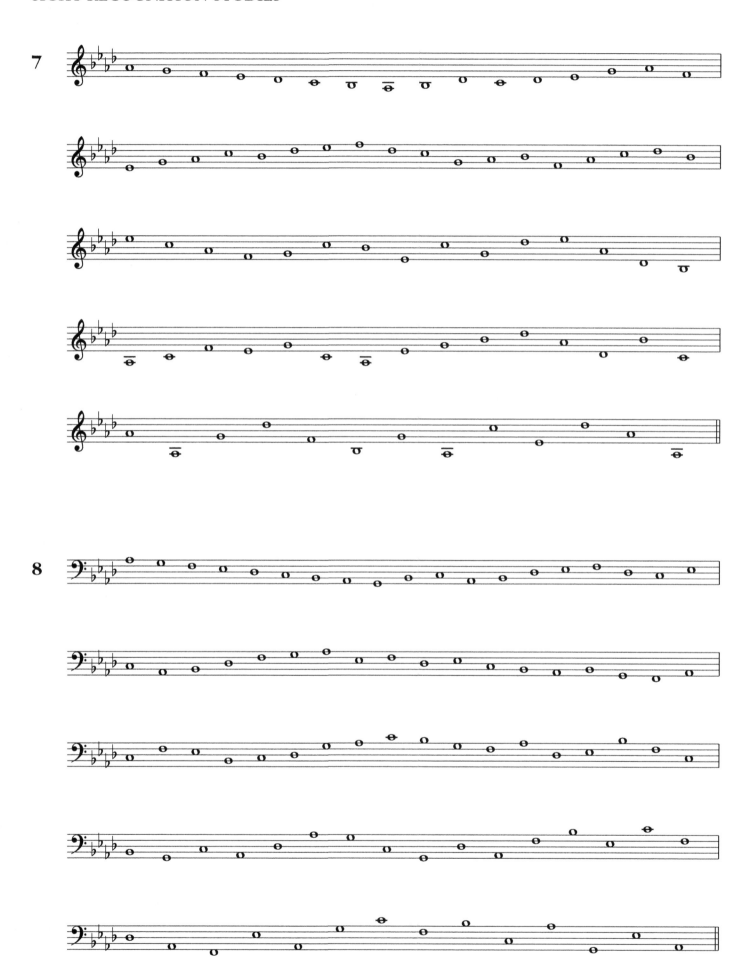

SOL-FA STUDIES

The following sol-fa studies, still in major, contain the challenge of singing melodic
motions in 4ths and 5ths. Remember to concentrate on the resolution of each note—not
the interval.

1   Do   Mi   Fa   Re   Mi   Do   Re   //   Do   Ti   Re

       Ti   Do   Re   Mi   //   Sol   Ti   La   Fa   Sol

       Fa   Mi   Do   Re   //   Do   La   Ti   Re   Do

2   Do   Re   Sol   //   La   Sol   Mi   //   Re   Do   Ti

       Do   Mi   Sol   Do   //   Re   Fa   Mi   Sol   Fa   La   Sol   //

       Ti   Do   Sol   Re   Mi   Ti   Do   Re   Do

3   Do   Re   Mi   La   Sol   Fa   Mi   //   Do   Fa   Mi

       Sol   La   Ti   Sol   //   Re   Do   Fa   Mi   La   Sol

       Fa   //   Mi   Do   Re   Fa   Do   Ti   Do   La   Do

Workshop Two
MELODIC STUDIES

Conduct and sing the following melodic studies. The new keys in this workshop are D, E♭, A, and A♭ major.

Workshop Two
MELODIC STUDIES

DUETS

17

18

The following studies utilize dotted-quarter- and eighth-note rhythms. See Lesson One
for a discussion of using subdivision in your conducting pattern.

45

Workshop Three

RHYTHMIC STUDIES

DUETS

Workshop Three

The following sight recognition exercises are in the keys of E, D♭, B, and G♭ major.
As you say the syllables for each note, try to keep steady time.

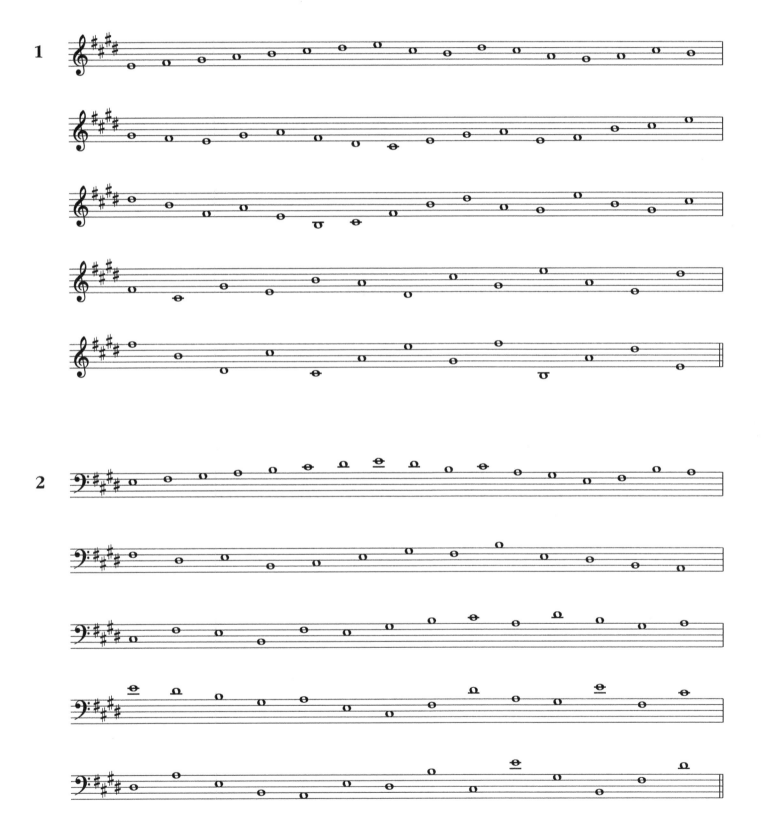

Workshop Three
SIGHT RECOGNITION STUDIES

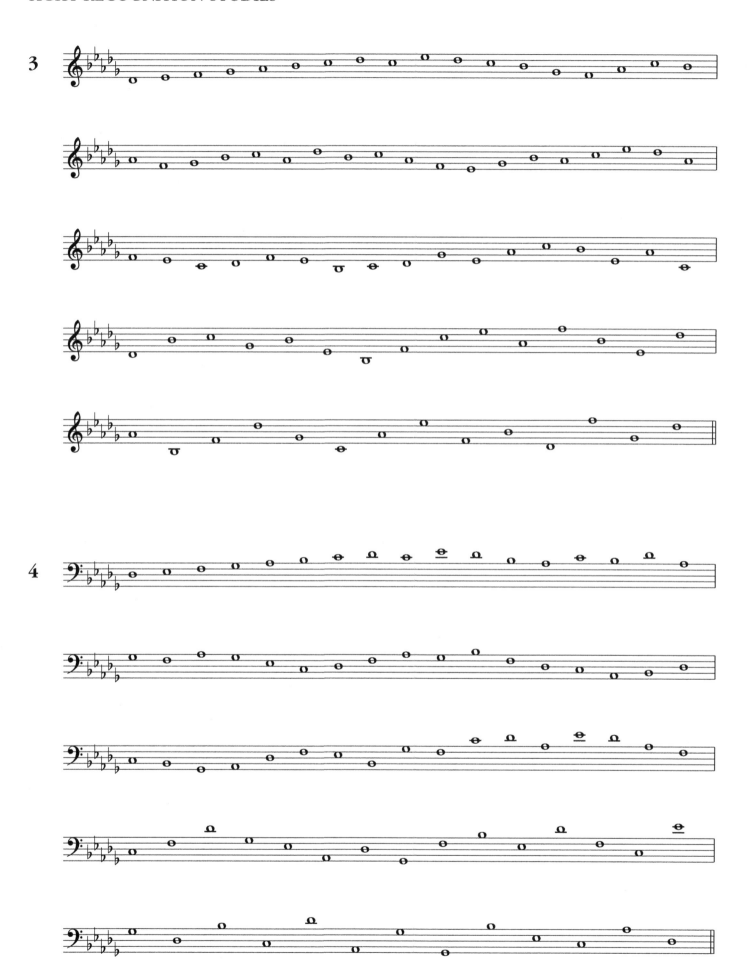

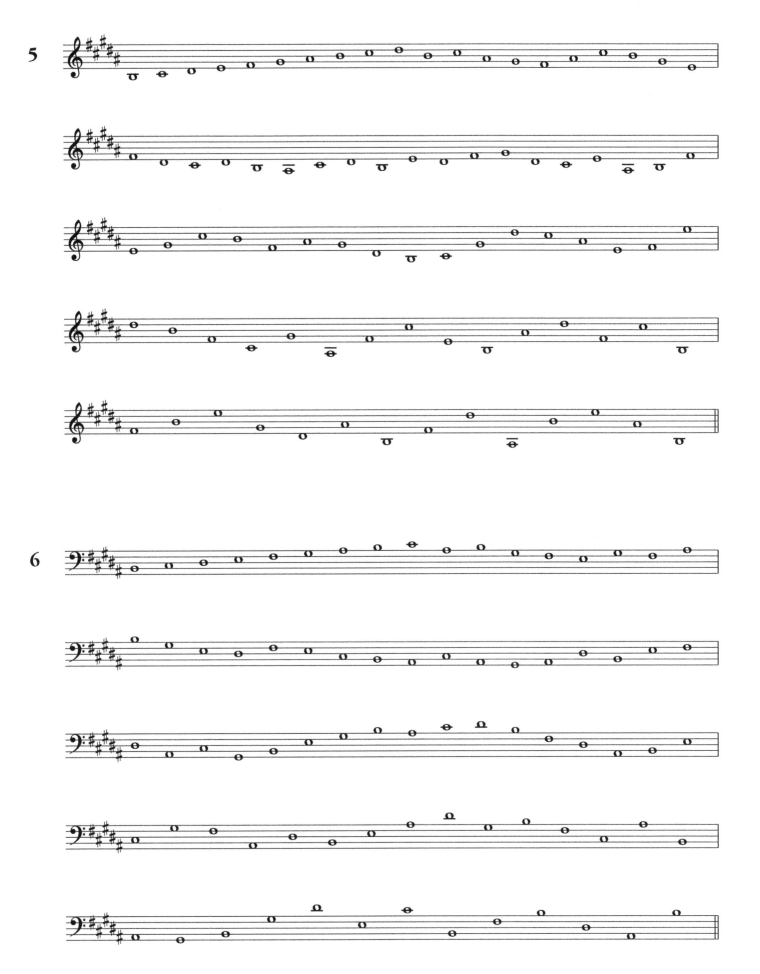

Workshop Three

SIGHT RECOGNITION STUDIES

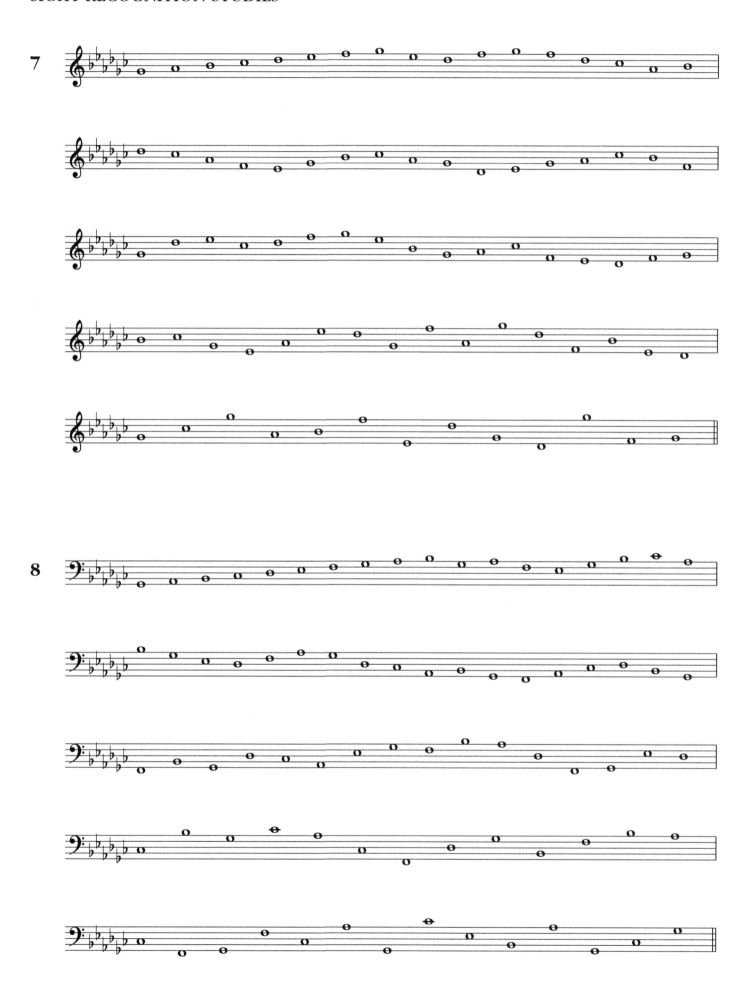

The sol-fa studies in this workshop contain many variations of melodic motion.

1   Do Mi Fa Sol Mi Ti Do // Fa Re Sol Fa Mi

      Ti Re // Mi Do La Sol Fa La Do // Ti Sol

      Fa La Sol Fa Re // Fa Do La Sol Ti Do

2   Sol Do Fa Mi Do La Re Sol // Fa Mi La

      Sol Re // Mi Ti Sol Re Fa La Re // Fa Mi

      Re La Sol // Ti La Fa Re Sol Fa Do

3   Do Sol La Mi Do La Re Mi Fa Do // La

      Ti Sol Ti Fa Mi Re Mi La Sol Re // Fa

      Mi Ti Do Fa Do Re La Sol Fa Ti Do Re Do

Workshop Three

MELODIC STUDIES

The following melodic studies add the keys of E, D♭, B and G♭ major, and contain melodic motion in 3rds. Be sure to conduct while singing the exercises.

Workshop Three

MELODIC STUDIES

DUETS

¢, 2/2 CONDUCTING PATTERN

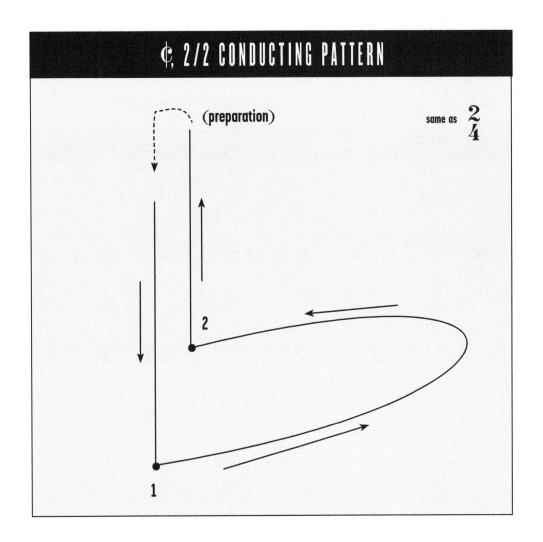

same as $\frac{2}{4}$

(preparation)

2

1

Conducting Hint:
When conducting time signatures where notes of relatively long duration get the pulse (as in 2/2 time), subdivide beats that have complex rhythms. Alternately when conducting a very slow 2/2, you can use a 4/4 pattern, emphasizing beats 1 and 3.

Workshop Four

RHYTHMIC STUDIES

The following rhythmic studies contain examples in cut time.

DUETS

Workshop Four

SIGHT RECOGNITION STUDIES

The following sight recognition studies are in the keys of F♯, C♭, and C♯ major.

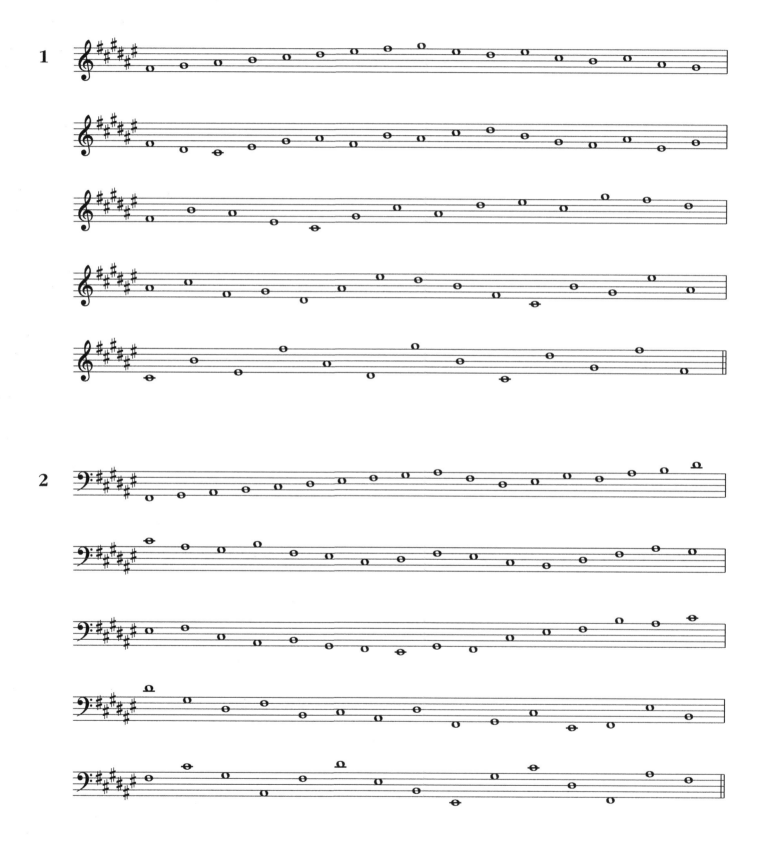

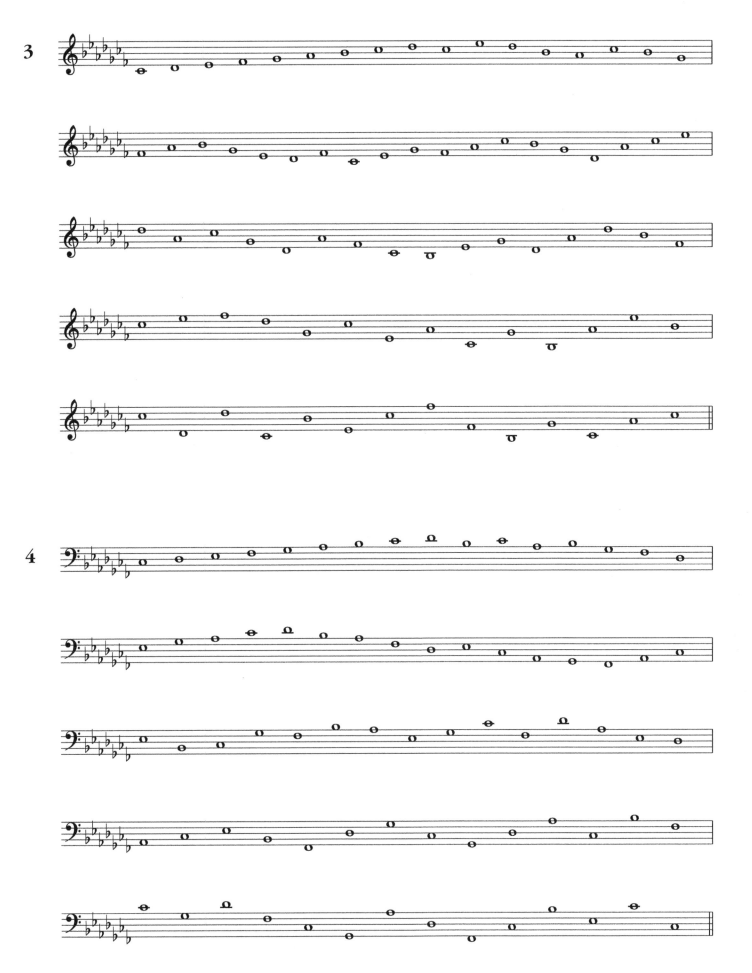

Workshop Four

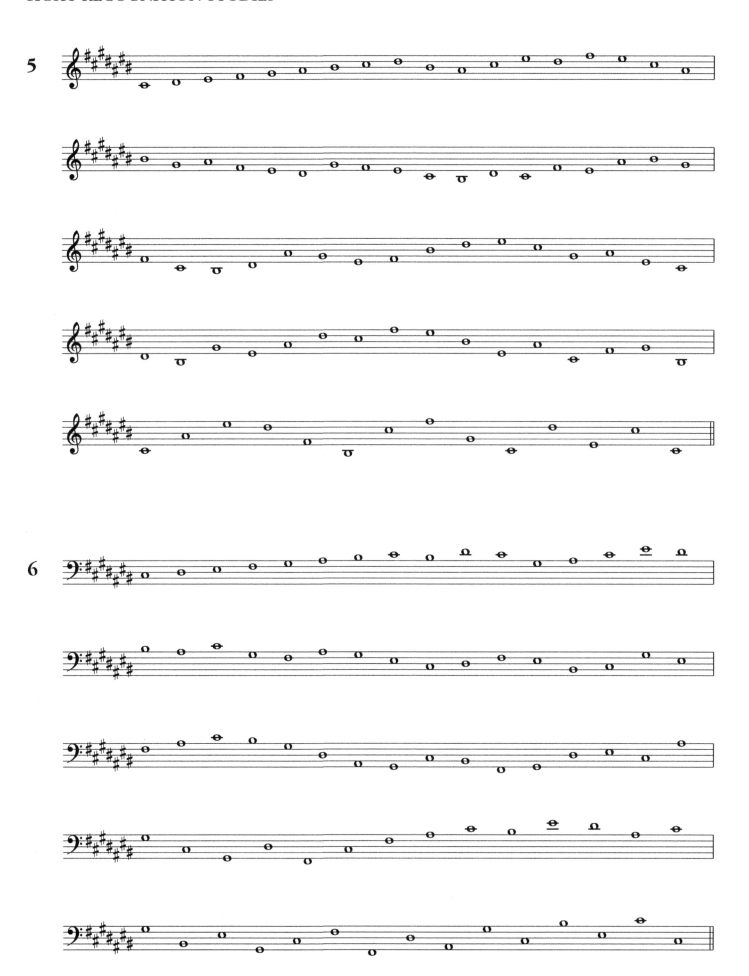

The sol-fa studies in this workshop focus on numerous and larger melodic jumps.
Choose the larger jumps when your vocal range allows. Remember to concentrate on
function (resolution), not interval motion.

1 Do Fa Re Sol Do // Mi Ti Re Fa Do //

La Fa Do Mi Sol Ti Re // Fa La Re

Sol Mi La Fa // Sol Mi Ti Fa Re Do

2 Sol Re Fa Mi Ti La Do // Mi La Re Sol

Do Mi La // Ti Fa Re La Sol Do Fa // Do

Mi Ti Re Fa // Sol Do Mi Ti Re La Do

3 Ti Mi Do La Re Sol Mi Do Fa // La Mi

Sol Re La Ti // Sol Fa Re La Ti Mi Re //

Do Sol Ti Fa La Mi Re La Sol Mi Do La Do

Workshop Four
MELODIC STUDIES

The melodic studies in this workshop add the keys of F♯, C♭, and C♯ major, and focus on melodic jumps and chordal motion.

Workshop Four

MELODIC STUDIES

18

DUETS

19

20

As with 2/2, the tempo of the example will determine the conducting pattern. Practice each of the new patterns both with their slow tempo and fast tempo patterns.

Slow Tempo	Fast Tempo

3/8 same as **3/4**

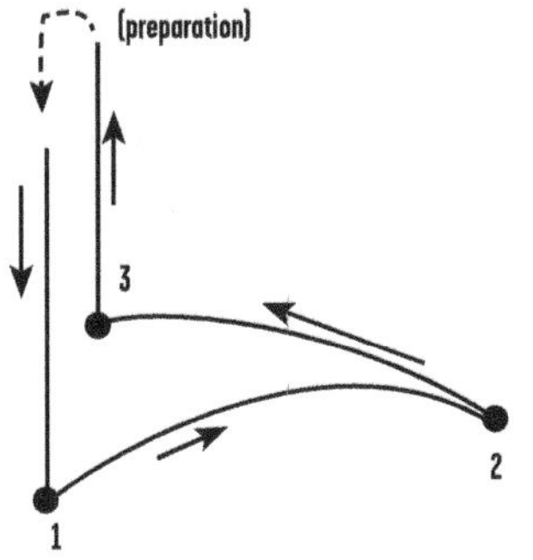

(preparation)

3

1   2

Fast Tempo: (preparation)

1

(one, two, three, one, two, three, etc.)

6/8

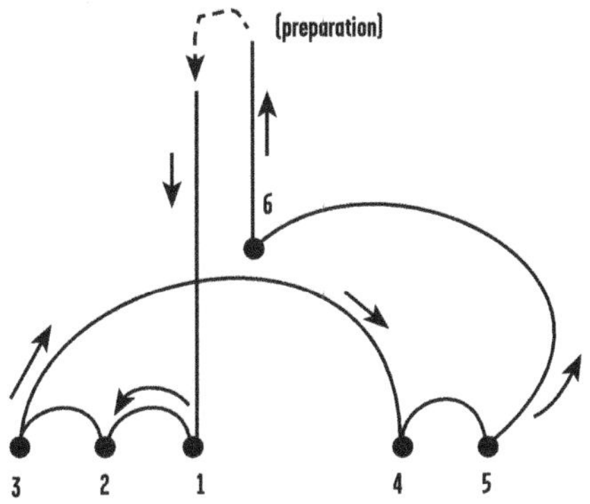

(preparation)

6

3 2 1   4 5

same as **2/4**

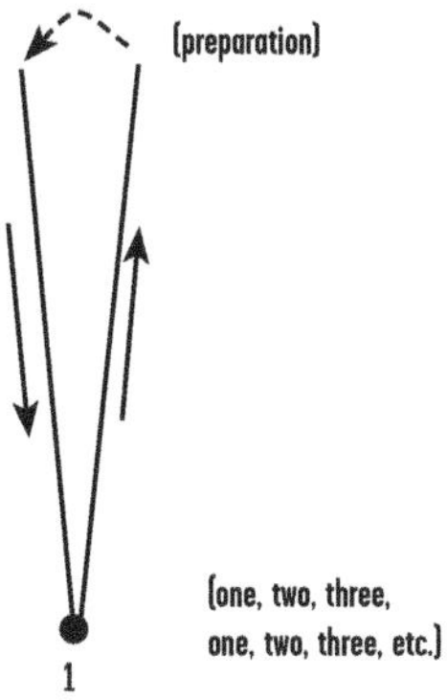

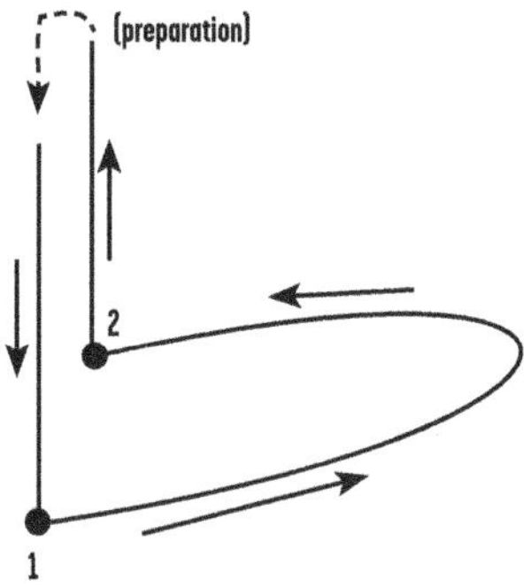

(preparation)

2

1

9/8

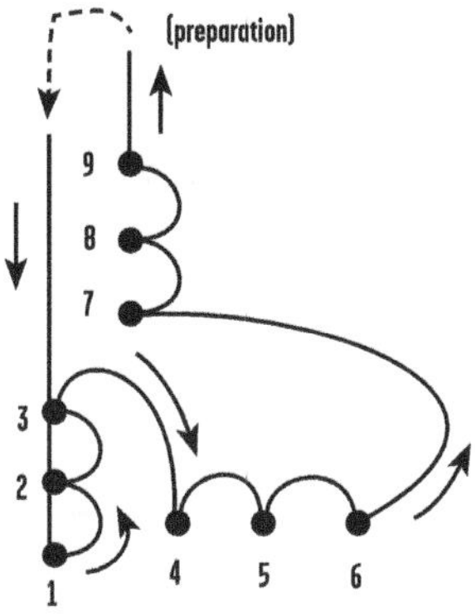

(preparation)

9 8 7

3 2 1   4 5 6

same as **3/4**

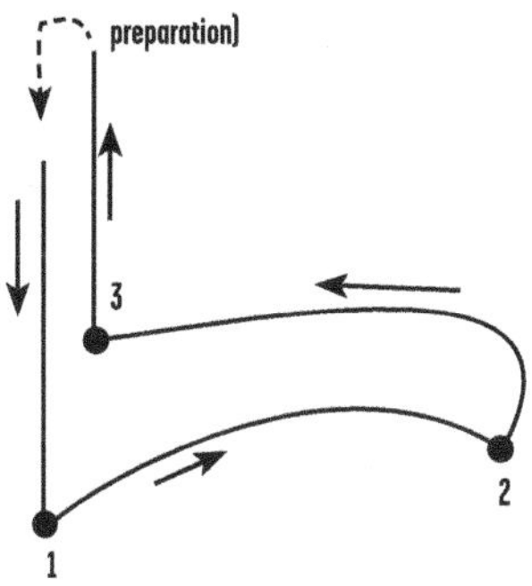

(preparation)

3

1   2

12/8

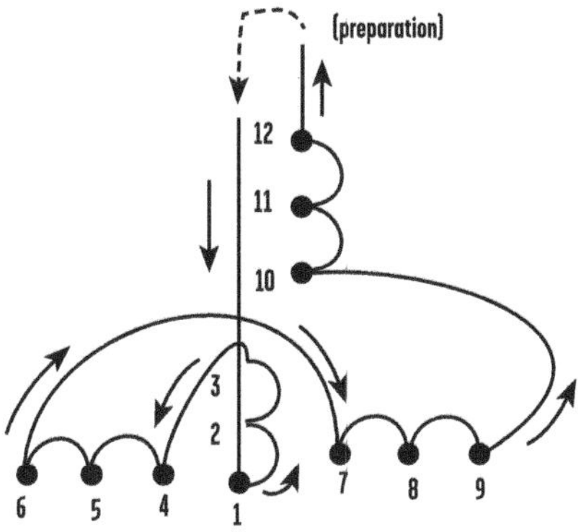

(preparation)

12 11 10

6 5 4 1   7 8 9

3 2

same as **4/4**

Start   (preparation)

4

2   1   3

65

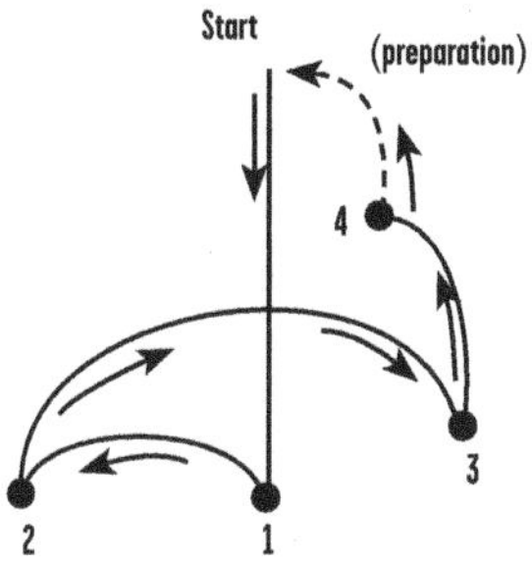

Workshop Five

RHYTHMIC STUDIES

The following rhythmic studies contain exercises in 3/8, 6/8, 9/8, and 12/8 time. Practice these examples at slow and steady tempos, utilizing the conducting patterns provided in this workshop. When you feel more comfortable with the exercises, experiment with faster tempi and use the alternate conducting pattern.

Workshop Five

RHYTHMIC STUDIES

DUETS

The following sight recognition exercises provide the opportunity to work in both major and minor keys. The accidentals in parentheses are to be used for minor-key sight recognition. Note: Exercise 1 gives you the option of practicing in the key of C major or A minor. For this exercise, the note G is Sol when singing in C major and the G♯ is Ti when singing in A minor. Practice these sight recognition exercises in both major and minor keys.

✗ = double sharp

69

Workshop Five
SIGHT RECOGNITION STUDIES

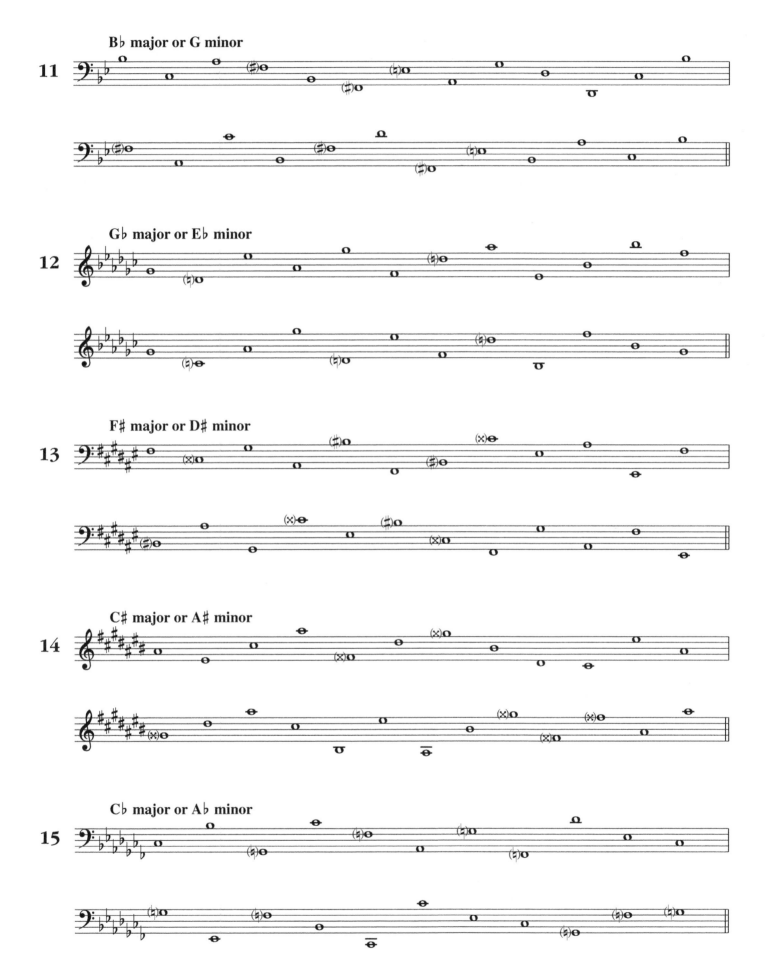

Workshop Five

SOL-FA STUDIES

The first few sol-fa studies in this workshop contain a lot of jumps. The rest of the exercises utilize three types of minor scales: traditional melodic, real, and harmonic.

1   Do Sol Re La Mi Ti Fa // Re Ti Mi La Re

    Sol Do // Fa Ti Sol Re La Mi Re // Sol Ti Re

    La Do // Fa Ti La Mi Sol Re Ti Mi Fa La Do

2   Do Mi Sol Ti La Fa Re Do Ti Re Fa La

    Sol Fa Mi // Fa La Do Mi Re Ti Sol Fa Mi

    Sol La // Ti Sol Mi Re Fa Re Do Ti Re Fa Do

3   Do Sol Mi Ti La Re Fa Do Re // Mi Ti Sol Re

    Mi La Do Sol Fa // Re La Fa Do Ti Fa

    Sol Re Mi // La Re Fa Do Ti Fa Sol Re Do

Three kinds of minor scales are used in the following exercises:

Traditional Melodic Minor								
Ascending	Do	Re	Me	Fa	Sol	La	Ti	Do
Descending	Do	Te	Le	Sol	Fa	Me	Re	Do
Real Minor								
	Do	Re	Me	Fa	Sol	Le	Te	Do
Harmonic Minor								
	Do	Re	Me	Fa	Sol	Le	Ti	Do

72

Traditional Melodic Minor

4 Do Re Me Fa Sol La Ti Do // Do Te Le Sol Fa Me Re Do //

Re Me Do Ti Do Re Me Sol // Fa Sol Le Sol Fa Me

Re Do Te Le Sol // Sol Me Ti Do Re Me Fa Sol La

Ti Do // Me Re Do Te Le Sol Fa Sol La Ti Do

Real minor

5 Do Re Me Fa Sol Le Te Do // Do Te La Sol Fa Me

Re Do // Do Me Fa Re Me Sol Le Do Te Le Sol

Fa Le Sol Te Do // Re Me Sol Le Fa Me Re Do //

Me Sol Le Te Re Do Sol // Le Te Do Re Do Te Do

Harmonic minor

6 Do Re Me Fa Sol Le Ti Do // Do Ti Le Sol Fa Me

Re Do // Re Me Fa Sol Le Sol Do // Ti Le Sol

Fa Sol Le Sol // Ti Do Re Me Re Ti Le // Sol

Fa Me Sol Le Ti Do // Me Re Fa Sol Le Ti Do

Workshop Five

MELODIC STUDIES

The following melodic studies contain exercises utilizing the major keys and time signatures used so far in this book. There are also exercises using the traditional melodic, real, and harmonic minor scales. Remember to conduct the time signature patterns as you sing the exercises.

Workshop Five

MELODIC STUDIES

The following rhythmic studies utilize the same time signatures that were previously covered, but provide an added challenge with the use of ties. Remember to keep a slow, steady tempo while reading and conducting these rhythms.

Workshop Six

RHYTHMIC STUDIES

DUETS

Workshop Six

SIGHT RECOGNITION STUDIES

The sight recognition studies in this workshop contain modes. The use of modes predates tonal concepts such as C major or D harmonic minor. We are not, however, studying modes for their historical importance, but rather because of their use in contemporary music. The following modes and many modal variations are commonly used in twentieth-century classical music, jazz, pop, folk, and world musics.

The following musical examples show how to practice the Dorian, Aeolian and Phrygian modes by starting with major scales and altering some of the notes.

Dorian Mode is similar to the real minor scale that you have already studied. Note the use of a ♭3rd (Me) and a ♭7th (Te) but, unlike real minor, the Dorian mode utilizes La rather than Le.

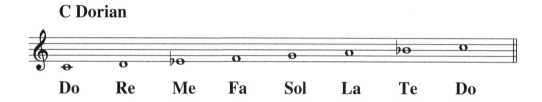

Aeolian Mode contains a ♭3rd, ♭6th, and ♭7th. Thus, it is just like real minor.

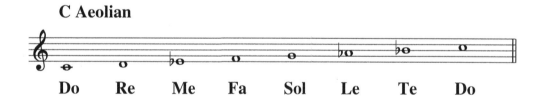

Phrygian Mode contains a ♭2nd, ♭3rd, ♭6th, and ♭7th. It is similar to real minor, but with the addition of the ♭2nd (Ra).

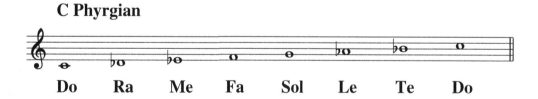

Figure 6.1. shows how you can practice Dorian, Aeolian, and Phrygian modes by using major scales.

Fig. 6.1.

CREATING MODES FROM MAJOR SCALES			
KEY	**DORIAN MODE**	**AEOLIAN MODE**	**PHRYGIAN MODE**
C	B♭ major scale starting on C	E♭ major scale starting on C	A♭ major scale starting on C
D	C major scale starting on D	F major scale starting on D	B♭ major scale starting on D
G	F major scale starting on G	B♭ major scale starting on G	E♭ major scale starting on G
A	G major scale starting on A	C major scale starting on A	F major scale starting on A
F	E♭ major scale starting on F	A♭ major scale starting on F	D♭ major scale starting on F
B♭	A♭ major scale starting on B♭	D♭ major scale starting on B♭	G♭ major scale starting on B♭
B	A major scale starting on B	D major scale starting on B	G major scale starting on B
E	D major scale starting on E	G major scale starting on E	C major scale starting on E
E♭	D♭ major scale starting on E♭	G♭ major scale starting on E♭	C♭ major scale starting on E♭
A♭	G♭ major scale starting on A♭	C♭ major scale starting on A♭	
F♯	E major scale starting on F♯	A major scale starting on F♯	D major scale starting on F♯
C♯	B major scale starting on C♯	E major scale starting on C♯	A major scale starting on C♯
D♭	C♭ major scale starting on D♭		
G♯	F♯ major scale starting on G♯	B major scale starting on G♯	E major scale starting on G♯
D♯	C♯ major scale starting on D♯	F♯ major scale starting on D♯	B major scale starting on D♯
A♯		C♯ major scale starting on A♯	F♯ major scale starting on A♯
E♯			C♯ major scale starting on E♯

Review the sight recognition exercises in Workshops 1–4 utilizing the Dorian, Aeolian, and Phrygian modes. Refer to Fig. 6.1. for assistance.

For example:

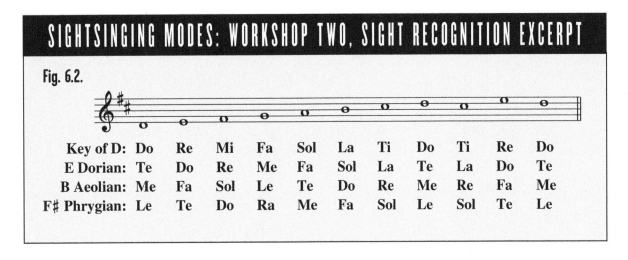

SIGHTSINGING MODES: WORKSHOP TWO, SIGHT RECOGNITION EXCERPT

Fig. 6.2.

Key of D:	Do	Re	Mi	Fa	Sol	La	Ti	Do	Ti	Re	Do
E Dorian:	Te	Do	Re	Me	Fa	Sol	La	Te	La	Do	Te
B Aeolian:	Me	Fa	Sol	Le	Te	Do	Re	Me	Re	Fa	Me
F♯ Phrygian:	Le	Te	Do	Ra	Me	Fa	Sol	Le	Sol	Te	Le

Workshop Six

SOL-FA STUDIES

The sol-fa studies in this workshop cover the minor scales and the Dorian, Aeolian, and Phrygian modes discussed in the sight recognition section of this workshop. Focus on the characteristic differences between the scales and the modes.

Traditional Minor

1 Do Me Fa Sol La Ti Do // Te Le Sol Le Sol Me

Re // Me Sol Ti Re Do Me Fa // Sol Le Fa Re

Ti Re Do // Me Sol Ti La Ti Do Re // Me

Do Te Sol Le Sol Fa // Sol Me Do Sol La Ti Do

Harmonic minor

2 Do Ti Le Sol Le Ti Re // Me Fa Le Sol Fa //

Me Re Fa Me Ti Le Sol // Le Ti Re Fa Me Re

Do // Le Fa Re Le Sol Me Do // Fa Le Sol Ti

Re Do Sol // Le Ti Le Sol Fa Me Do Ti Le Sol Do

Real minor (also Aeolian)

3   Do Me Sol Te Le Sol Fa Le Sol Me Do Re Me //

Fa Le Do Re Te Do Sol // Le Fa Sol Te Re Do //

Fa Sol Le Fa Me Do Le // Te Sol Me Do Re //

Me Do Sol Le Te Re Me // Sol Le Te Sol Me Do

Dorian

4   Do Re Me Fa Sol La Te Do // Do Te La Sol Fa Me

Re Do // Me Fa Sol La Sol La Te // Do Re Do Sol

La Te La // Sol Fa Me Do Te Re Te // Do Re Me

Sol La Te Do // Me Re Te Re Do La Sol Te Do

Phrygian

5   Do Ra Me Fa Sol Le Te Do // Do Te Le Sol Fa Me

Ra Do // Ra Me Ra Me Do Te Do // Sol Me Ra Me

Do Sol Le Te Do // Ra Me Fa Ra Me Sol Le // Te

Do Ra Te Le Te Do // Ra Fa Sol Te Le Sol Ra Do

Workshop Six

MELODIC STUDIES

The melodic studies in this workshop review the minor scales and the Dorian, Aeolian, and Phrygian modes learned in the sol-fa studies section of this workshop. Remember to conduct while reading these exercises.

Workshop Six

MELODIC STUDIES

Workshop Seven

RHYTHMIC STUDIES

The rhythmic studies in this workshop utilize sixteenth notes and rests. Remember to read these examples at slow, steady tempos while conducting. See Lesson One for a review about subdivision and conducting.

Workshop Seven

RHYTHMIC STUDIES

DUETS

Workshop Seven

SIGHT RECOGNITION STUDIES

The sight recognition studies in this workshop contain two more modes. Fig. 7.3. shows how you can practice the Mixolydian and Lydian modes using major scales.

Mixolydian Mode is similar to a major scale except for a ♭7th (Te).

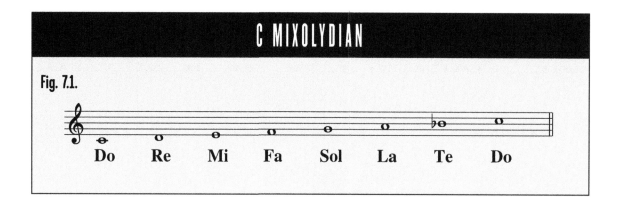

Lydian Mode is also similar to the major scale except for a ♯4 (Fi).

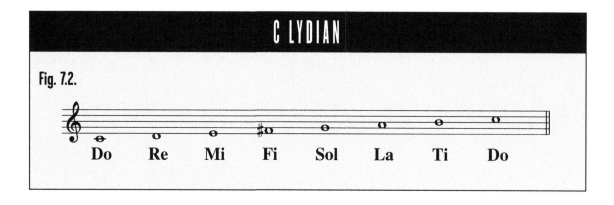

Fig. 7.3.

CREATING MORE MODES FROM MAJOR SCALES

KEY	MIXOLYDIAN MODE	LYDIAN MODE
G	C major scale starting on G	D major scale starting on G
C	F major scale starting on C	G major scale starting on C
D	G major scale starting on D	A major scale starting on D
F	B♭ major scale starting on F	C major scale starting on F
A	D major scale starting on A	E major scale starting on A
B♭	E♭ major scale starting on B♭	F major scale starting on B♭
E	A major scale starting on E	B major scale starting on E
E♭	A♭ major scale starting on E♭	B♭ major scale starting on E♭
B	E major scale starting on B	F♯ major scale starting on B
A♭	D♭ major scale starting on A♭	E♭ major scale starting on A♭
F♯	B major scale starting on F♯	C♯ major scale starting on F♯
D♭	G♭ major scale starting on D♭	A♭ major scale starting on D♭
C♯	F♯ major scale starting on C♯	
G♭	C♭ major scale starting on G♭	D♭ major scale starting on G♭
G♯	C♯ major scale starting on G♯	
F♭		C♭ major scale starting on F♭
C♭		G♭ major scale starting on C♭

SIGHTSINGING MODES: WORKSHOP SEVEN, SIGHT RECOGNITION EXCERPT

Fig. 7.4.

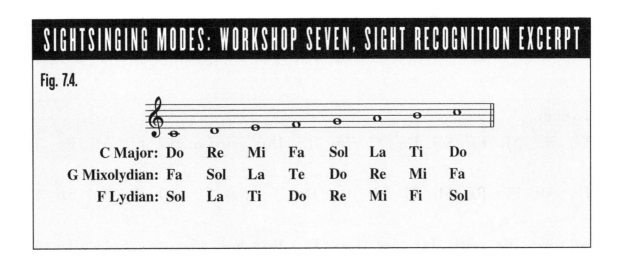

C Major:	Do	Re	Mi	Fa	Sol	La	Ti	Do
G Mixolydian:	Fa	Sol	La	Te	Do	Re	Mi	Fa
F Lydian:	Sol	La	Ti	Do	Re	Mi	Fi	Sol

Workshop Seven

SOL-FA STUDIES

The sol-fa studies in this workshop contain exercises in the Mixolydian and Lydian modes. They also contain major scale exercises (also known as the Ionian mode) for comparison.

Ionian (Major)

1   Do Mi Sol Ti La Fa Sol Re Mi Do // Sol Ti Re

     Fa Mi Ti Re // La Sol Mi Fa Do Mi La Re Sol

     Fa La Do Re Sol Ti Fa // Mi Sol Re La Mi Ti

     Re // Fa Ti Mi La Re Sol Ti Fa Do Sol La Re Do

Mixolydian

2   Do Re Mi Fa Sol La Te Do // Do Te La Sol Fa Mi Re Do //

     Do Mi Sol La Te Sol Do // Re Te La Te Do Sol Do //

     Mi Sol La Te Sol Mi Do Te Re // Mi Sol La Te Do Re

     Te Do // Sol Te La Fa Sol La Sol Mi Te Re Mi Te Do

Lydian

3   Do Re Mi Fi Sol La Ti Do // Do Ti La Sol Fi Mi Re Do //

     Do Mi Fi Re Mi Fi Mi Re Do // Sol Fi Mi Fi Sol Mi Do //

     Mi Fi Re Mi Fi Sol La Ti Do Sol Fi // Sol Mi Fi Re

     Do Ti Do // Mi Fi La Sol Fi Re Do // La Fi Sol La Do Re Do

Workshop Seven
MELODIC STUDIES

The melodic studies in this workshop review the major scale (Ionian mode) as well as introduce Mixolydian and Lydian modes.

Workshop Seven

MELODIC STUDIES

Workshop Seven
MELODIC STUDIES

Workshop Eight

RHYTHMIC STUDIES

The rhythmic studies in this workshop focus on sixteenth-note rests and isolated sixteenth notes. Isolated notes, like tied notes, require you to concentrate on what's *not* being sung. So, a strong conducting pattern and use of subdivision will help you a lot. Go slowly and concentrate on the beats and subdivisions.

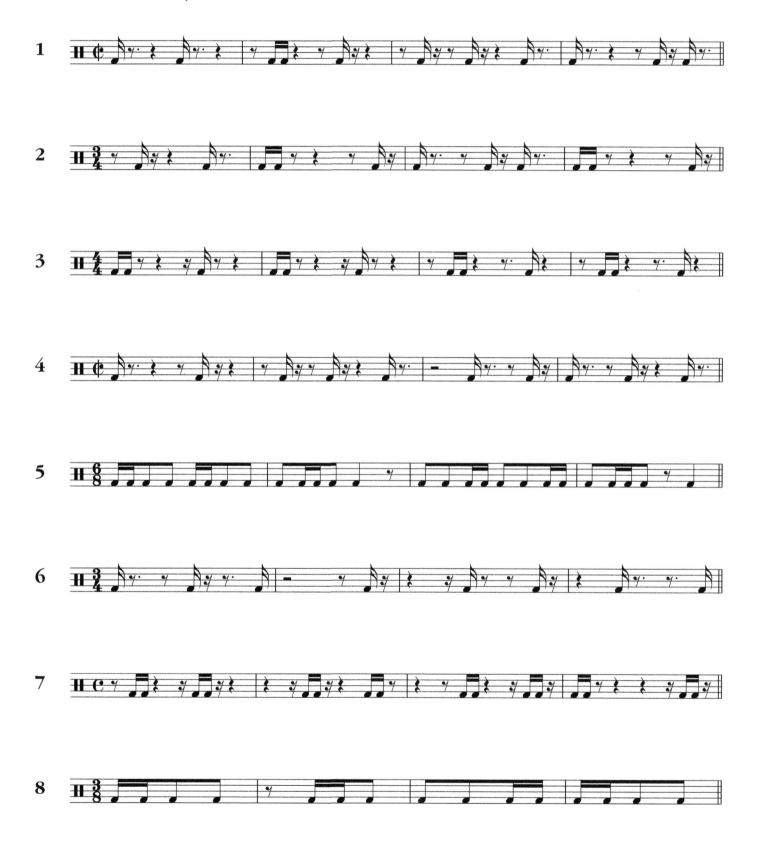

Workshop Eight

RHYTHMIC STUDIES

DUETS

Workshop Eight

SIGHT RECOGNITION STUDIES

The following sight recognition studies use mixed modality. Simply put, mixed modality combines the various solfège functions found in major and minor scales along with the five modes you have studied.

Note that the melodic changes you see are all stepwise. They should be said just as they appear.

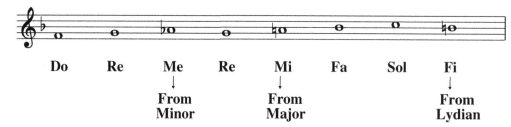

Do	Re	Me	Re	Mi	Fa	Sol	Fi
		↓		↓			↓
		From		From			From
		Minor		Major			Lydian

The purpose of mixed modal studies is to prepare you for tonal chromaticism, which you will study in upcoming workshops.

Workshop Eight

SOL-FA STUDIES

The following sol-fa exercises contain mixed modality. See the sight recognition studies in this workshop for a discussion of mixed modality.

1   Do Re Mi Fa Me Re Do // Do Ti Do Re Do Te Do //

Sol La Sol Fa Sol Le Sol // Sol La Te Do Re Do Ti //

Do Sol Fa Sol Fi Mi Re // Do Re Me Fa Me Ra Do //

Re Mi Fi Sol La Sol Fa // Mi Fa Me Re Do Te Do

2   Do Ti La Sol Le Te Do // Ti La Sol Fa Sol Le Sol //

Le Te Do Re Mi Re Do // Ra Me Fa Sol Fa Me Re //

Do Re Mi Sol La Te La // Sol Fi Mi Re Mi Fa Sol //

Le Te Le Sol Fa Sol La // Ti Do Ra Me Fa Mi Re Do

3   Do Mi Fi Sol Le Sol La Te Do Re Do Ti Le // Sol Fi Mi

Re Me Re Do Te Do // Ra Me Fa Sol La Ti Do Ti Le Sol

Fa Me Fa // Sol Fi Mi Re Me Re Do Ti Do Ra Me Re

Do // Te La Ti Do Te Le Te Do Ti La Sol Le Ti Re Do

4   Sol Fi Mi Do Re Me Fa   //   Sol La Te Le Sol Fa Mi   //

Re Do Ti Do Te Le Sol La Sol   //   Fi Mi Fa Me Re

Mi Re Me Ra Do Ti Do Te Le Te Do Ti La Sol   //

Le Te La Ti Do Re Do Ra Me Fa Mi Fi Sol Mi Do

5   Do Re Mi Re Do   //   Do Ra Mi Ra Do   //   Do Ti Le Sol Fa

Do Ti Le Sol Fi Sol Do   //   Do Ra Mi Fi Sol Le Ti Do   //

Do Ti Le Sol Fi Mi Ra Do   //   Do Ra Mi Fi Sol La Te

Do   //   Do Te La Sol Fi Mi Ra Do   //   Mi Ra Do Sol Le Ti Do

6   Do Re Me Fa Me Re Do   //   Do Re Me Fi Me Re Do   //

Do Ti Le Sol Fi Me Re Do   //   Re Me Fi Sol Le Ti Do   //

Do Re Me Fi Sol Fi Me Ra Do   //   Ra Me Fi Sol La Te Do   //

Ti Le Sol Fi Me Re Me   //   Fi Me Ra Do Ti La Do

Workshop Eight
MELODIC STUDIES

The following melodic studies contain major key signatures with modal accidentals. Remember to think of the melodic changes as modal or stepwise. Note that in most examples, you will be comparing one modal phrase to another.

Workshop Eight

MELODIC STUDIES

Workshop Nine
RHYTHMIC STUDIES

The rhythmic studies in this workshop continue to review isolated sixteenth notes in all time signatures. Many of the exercises contain the added challenge of sixteenth notes with ties. As with the exercises in Workshop Eight, concentrate on your beat (conducting pattern) and subdivisions. This will help you to make accurate articulations and count through the rests. Remember to give full value to your durations, especially those with ties.

Workshop Nine

RHYTHMIC STUDIES

Workshop Nine
RHYTHMIC STUDIES

DUETS

Workshop Nine

RHYTHMIC STUDIES

18

19

The following sight recognition exercises contain stepwise chromaticism in the keys of C, F, B♭, E♭, G, D, A, and E major. Remember to identify the chromatic notes by their function, i.e., their expected resolution. For example, in Exercise 1, F♯ is an ascending chromatic in the key of C and is expected to resolve (theoretically) to the note G. Thus, F♯ should be identified as Fi.

Workshop Nine
SIGHT RECOGNITION STUDIES

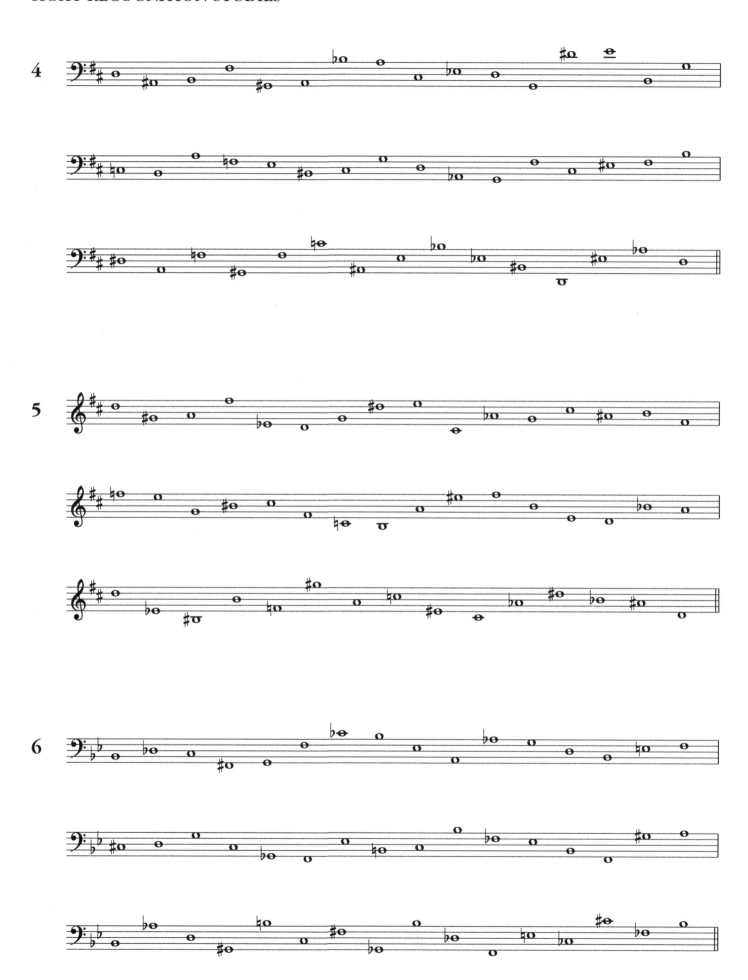

Workshop Nine

SIGHT RECOGNITION STUDIES

10

11

12

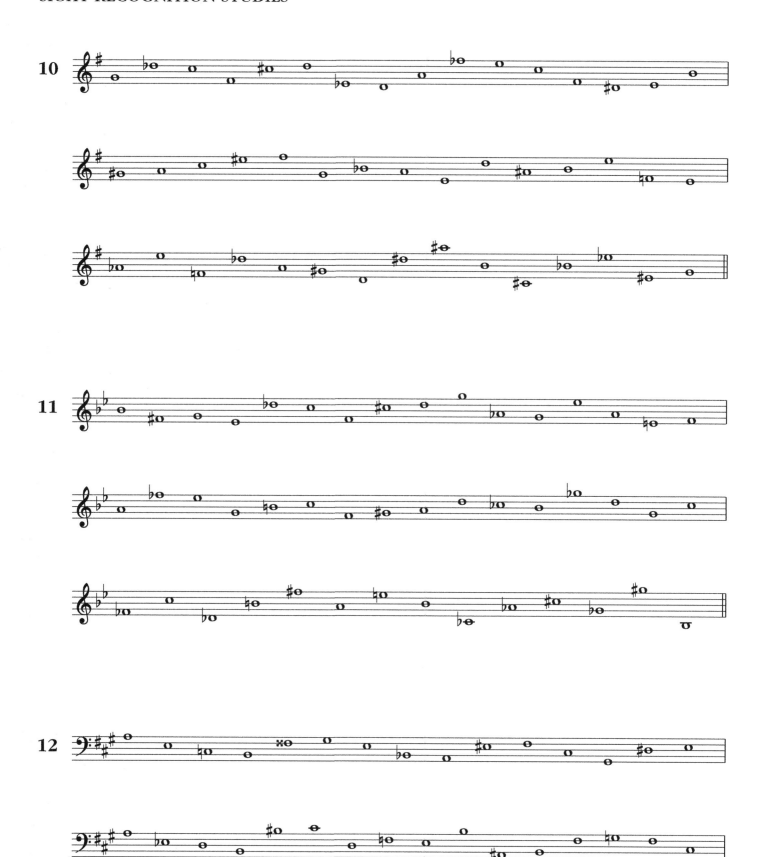

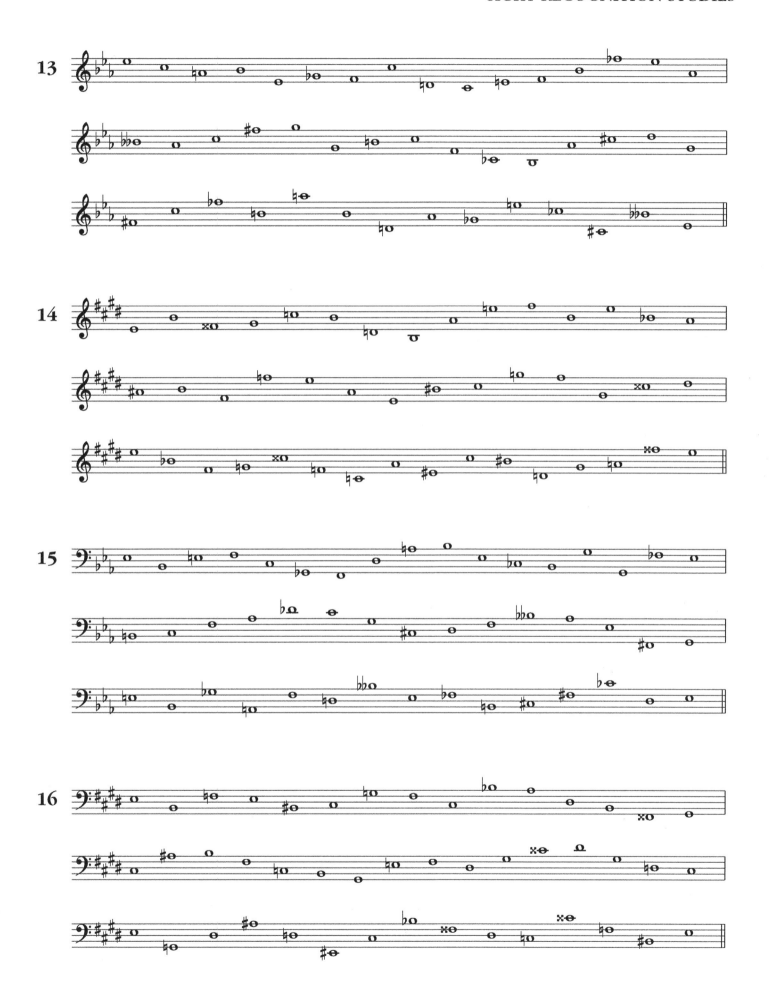

Workshop Nine

SOL-FA STUDIES

The sol-fa studies in this workshop contain more practice with stepwise chromaticism. It is important to sing the chromatic notes in tune. It is quite easy to lose your sense of key or Do. Go slowly through the exercises. Put space or silence between each note. This will help you develop your inner hearing of the notes.

Note that the first part of Exercise 1 features a chromatic scale, up and down. Consider practicing this exercise a number of times until you feel confident about your intonation.

1   Do Di Re Ri Mi Fa Fi Sol Si La Li Ti Do // Do Ti Te

       La Le Sol Se Fa Mi Me Re Ra Do // Do Re Ri Mi Fa

       Mi Re Do // Do Di Re Mi Fa Me Re Do // Do Ti Te

       La Sol La Ti Do // Do Ti La Le Sol La Ti Do

2   Do Re Mi Fa Fi Sol La Ti Do // Do Ti La Sol Se

       Fa Mi Fa Sol Do // Re Mi Sol Si La Ti La Sol //

       Fa Mi Me Re Do Re Mi // Do Ti La Le Sol La

       Ti Do Ti Te La Le Sol Fa // Mi Me Re Ra Do Ti Do

3   Do Ti Li Ti Do Ti La Sol // Fa Mi Ri Mi Fa Mi Re //

       Do Re Me Re Mi Sol La // La Si La Ti Do Ra Do //

       Sol Fi Sol La Sol Fa Mi Ri Mi Re Do Ti La Le

       Sol // Se Fa Mi Fa Fi Sol La // Si La Li Ti Re Ra Do

4   Do La Sol Fi Sol Fa Mi ⁄⁄ Ri Mi Sol La Fa Mi Re ⁄⁄

    Ri Mi Sol Se Fa La Sol ⁄⁄ Si La Ti Re Me Re Do ⁄⁄

    Re Mi Sol Le Sol La Ti Re Do Di Re Fa Mi Ri Mi ⁄⁄

    Fa Fi Sol Le Sol La Te La Sol La Ti Re Di Re Do

5   Do Mi Sol Se Fa Mi Ri Mi Re ⁄⁄ Fa Se Fa Re Mi Fa

    Sol Si La Ti Sol Fi Sol ⁄⁄ Ti Re Do Re Do Ti

    Li Ti La Si La Sol Mi Ri Mi ⁄⁄ Fa Mi Me Re

    Mi Sol La Sol Fa Se Fa Re Mi Ri Mi Me Re Do

6   Sol Si La Te La Si La ⁄⁄ Sol Fa Fi Sol La Te La ⁄⁄

    Ti Re Me Re Do Re Mi Sol ⁄⁄ Ti Li Ti La Sol Se

    Fa ⁄⁄ Do Ra Do Sol Mi Ri Mi La Fa Se Fa Re Mi

    Fa Sol ⁄⁄ Ti Li Ti La Sol La Te La Sol Fi Sol

    Fa Re Di Re Ti Do Ra Do Ti Te La Do

Workshop Nine

MELODIC STUDIES

The melodic studies in this workshop contain stepwise chromaticism in various major and minor keys. At this point, the chromatic notes are doing what they are "supposed to" theoretically... that is, resolve to the expected diatonic note, i.e., Fi to Sol, Me to Re, and so on.

Remember to identify the notes as they read, i.e., F♯ is Fi in the key of C. As you hear the chromatic notes, try to imagine their "expected" resolution. This will help you to sing the chromatic notes in tune.

Workshop Nine
MELODIC STUDIES

16

CHROMATIC DUETS

17

18

The rhythmic studies in this workshop utilize quarter-note triplets. The following directions will help you sing quarter-note triplets using eighth-note triplets as your reference.

1. First, sing the eighth-note triplets using "1, 2, 1, 2, etc."

2. Next, try to accent only the "1s" (this will let you begin to hear how the quarter-note triplets sound).

3. Gradually, drop the "2s" altogether, singing only the "1s." You are now singing quarter-note triplets. Make sure that you sing full value for each quarter-note triplet (now that you have dropped the "2s").

Workshop Ten
RHYTHMIC STUDIES

Workshop Ten

RHYTHMIC STUDIES

DUETS

The following sight recognition exercises continue the stepwise chromaticism from Workshop Nine in the keys of A♭, D♭, G♭, C♭, B, F♯ and C major. You will also see some chromatic notes that don't resolve (either immediately or ever). Make sure to sing these as they function by virtue of the expected chromatic resolution. For example, F♯ is still Fi in the key of C, whether it resolves to the note G or not.

Workshop Ten
SIGHT RECOGNITION STUDIES

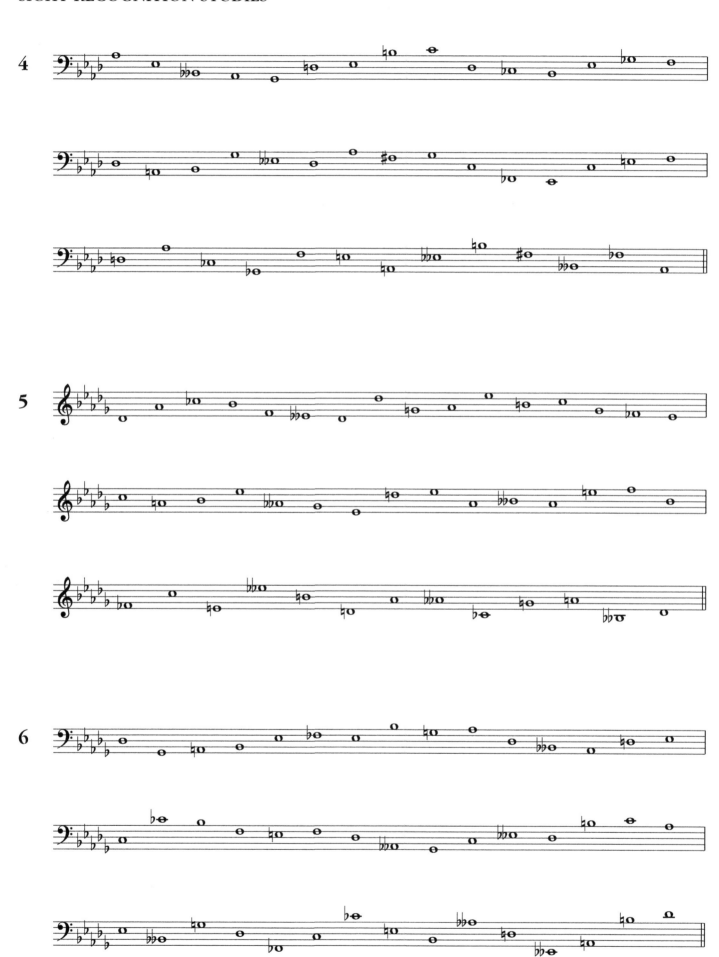

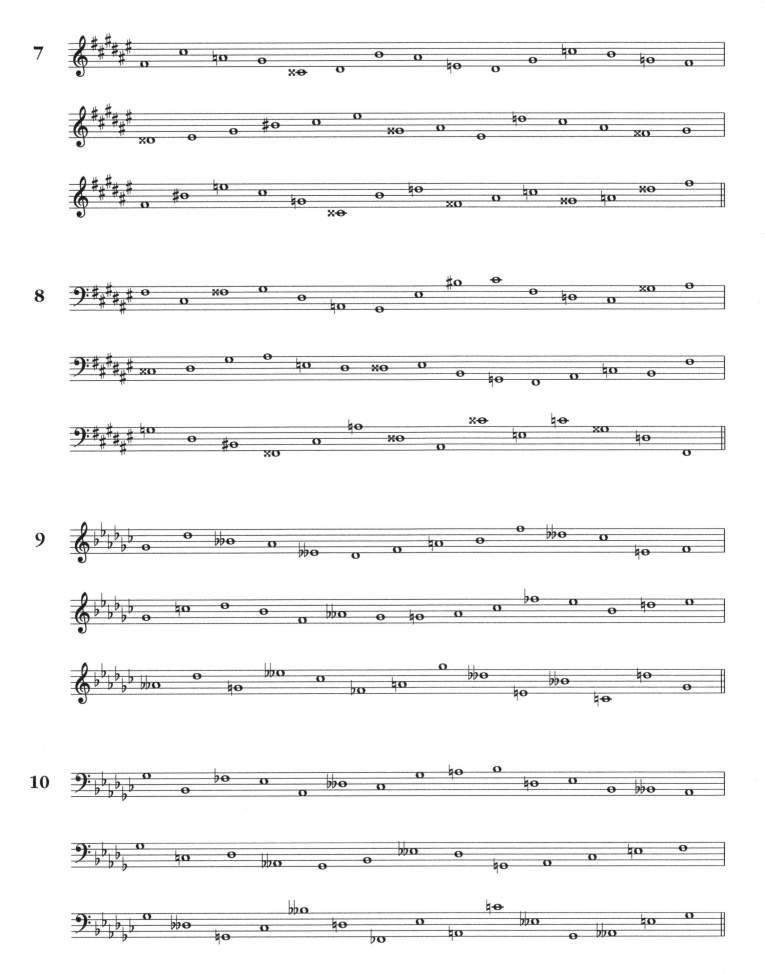

Workshop Ten
SIGHT RECOGNITION STUDIES

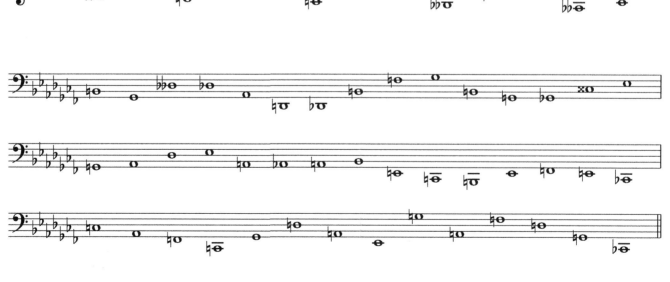

The sol-fa studies in this workshop utilize stepwise chromaticism, diatonic jumps to chromatic notes, and stepwise resolution. Note that the diatonic jumps to chromatic notes are often "prepared" by a stepwise resolution immediately before the jump.

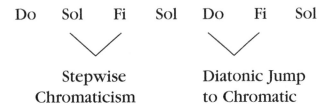

This exercise suggests a way to practice chromatics that are "jumped to," or as they are often called, "unprepared" chromatics.

For example, suppose you have the following chromatic jump to read:

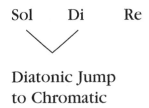

The way to practice this jump would be to sing the following, either in your mind or out loud:

Sol   Re   Di   Re   Sol   Re   Di   Re   Sol   Di   Re

Stepwise   Stepwise   Jump

Workshop Ten

SOL-FA STUDIES

1 Do Ti Li Ti La Sol Se Fa Mi Me Re // Mi Fa Se Fa

Sol Mi Re Di Re // Do La Si La Ti Sol Se Fa Mi Sol

Le // Sol Se Fa Mi Ti Te La Li // Ti Do Sol Fa Se Fa

Mi Me // Re Mi Fa Fi Sol Le Sol Se // Fa Mi Do Ra Do

2 Do Mi La Te La Sol Mi Ri Mi Re // Fa Se Fa Re Di

Re Mi Sol Si La // Ti Do Sol Fi Sol Le Sol Fa Re

Ra Do // Ra Do Re La Si La Sol Ti Re // Me Re Mi

Ti Li Ti La Sol Fa Se Fa Sol Mi Ri Mi Re Do

3 Do Sol Fi Sol Do Fi Sol // Fa Mi Sol Do Ra Do

Sol Ra Do // Ti Do Mi Ri Mi Do Ri Mi Re // Sol

Le Sol Do Le Sol Fa // Sol Fi Sol Mi Do Fi Sol //

Re Me Re Do Me Re Do // Re Mi Ri Mi Do Ri Mi Do

4   Do Mi Fa Se Fa Do Se Fa // Sol Mi Re Di Re Mi Di

Re // Do La Si La Do Si La // Sol La Te La Sol Te

La Ti Do // Do Ra Do Sol Ra Do Re // Fa Mi Sol

Fi Sol Re Fi Sol Fa // Mi Do Ti Li Ti Sol Li Ti Do

5   Do La Si La Do Si La Sol Mi // Re Fa Se Fa Re Se

Fa Mi // Sol La Te La Sol Te La Sol // Re Di Re Sol

Di Re Mi // Fa Sol Ti Li Ti Sol Li Ti La Sol Re

Me Re Sol Me Re Mi Fa // Sol Le Sol Fa Le Sol Do

6   Do La Mi Ri Mi La Ri Mi // Fa La Fa Se Fa La

Se Fa // Mi Re Sol Fi Sol Re Fi Sol Fa // Mi Fa

Do Ra Do Fa Ra Do Re Sol // Mi La Te La Mi

Te La Sol Ti Re // Mi Ti Li Ti Ti Li Ti Re Do

Workshop Ten

MELODIC STUDIES

The melodic studies in this workshop review stepwise chromaticism, diatonic jumps to chromatic notes, and stepwise resolution. Remember to concentrate on the chromatic resolution to the diatonic note when you have a stepwise chromatic.

When you have a diatonic jump to a chromatic, think of the resolution in your head. Don't try to measure the jump by interval. Concentrate on the expected resolution. This will help you to develop an accurate, long-term memory of the chromatic functions.

132

Workshop Ten

MELODIC STUDIES

Workshop Ten
MELODIC STUDIES

DUETS

31

32

ABOUT THE AUTHOR

Steve Prosser is Chair of the Ear Training Department at Berklee College of Music in Boston, where he has taught since 1979. He is a noted studio vocalist, pianist, arranger and producer. Prosser received his Ph.D. from Boston College and his J.D. from Suffolk University Law School. He is an attorney and member of the Massachusetts Bar.

Berklee Press

Your Resource for Composing, Arranging, and Improvising Music!

ARRANGING FOR HORNS
by Jerry Gates
Write for a horn section! In this book, you will learn how to add saxophones and brass to a rhythm section ensemble.
00121625 Book/Online Audio $19.99

ARRANGING FOR LARGE JAZZ ENSEMBLE
by Dick Lowell and Ken Pullig
Learn the same jazz ensemble arranging techniques taught by renowned Berklee College of Music faculty.
50449528 Book/CD Pack $39.99

ARRANGING FOR STRINGS
by Mimi Rabson
Presenting time-tested techniques and contemporary developments in writing and arranging for strings. You'll learn strategies for authentic writing in many different styles.
00190207 Book/Online Audio $19.99

THE BERKLEE BOOK OF JAZZ HARMONY
by Joe Mulholland & Tom Hojnacki
This text provides a strong foundation in harmonic principles, supporting further study in jazz composition, arranging, and improvisation.
00113755 Book/Online Audio $27.50

BERKLEE CONTEMPORARY MUSIC NOTATION
by Jonathan Feist
Learn the nuances of music notation, and create professional looking scores.
00202547 .... $17.99

BERKLEE MUSIC THEORY – 2ND EDITION
by Paul Schmeling
This method features rigorous, hands-on, "ears-on" practice exercises that help you explore the inner working of music. Book 2 focuses on harmony.
50449615 Book 1: Book/Online Audio $24.99
50449616 Book 2: Book/Online Audio $22.99

BLUES IMPROVISATION COMPLETE
by Jeff Harrington
Learn to improvise in jazz, Latin, fusion, blues and rock styles in all keys with step-by-step instructions and play-along audio.
50449486 Bb Instruments: Book/Online Audio $22.99
50449425 C Instruments: Book/Online Audio $22.99
50449487 Eb Instruments: Book/Online Audio $22.99

COMPLETE GUIDE TO FILM SCORING – 2ND EDITION
by Richard Davis
Learn the art and business of film scoring, including: the film-making process, preparing and recording a score, contracts and fees, publishing, royalties, and copyrights.
50449607 Book $29.99

CONTEMPORARY COUNTERPOINT
by Beth Denisch
Use counterpoint to make your music more engaging and creative. You will learn "tricks of the trade" from the masters and apply these skills to contemporary styles.
00147050 Book/Online Audio $22.99

A GUIDE TO JAZZ IMPROVISATION
by John LaPorta
Berklee Professor Emeritus John LaPorta's method provides a practical and intuitive approach to teaching basic jazz improvisation through 12 lessons and accompanying audio.
50449439 C Instruments: Book/Online Audio $19.99
50449441 Bb Instruments: Book/Online Audio $19.99
50449442 Eb Instruments: Book/Online Audio $19.99
50449443 BC Instruments: Book/Online Audio $19.99

IMPROVISATION FOR CLASSICAL MUSICIANS
by Eugene Friesen with Wendy M. Friesen
Learn the creative mindset and acquire the technical tools necessary for improvisation.
50449637 Book/CD Pack $24.99

JAZZ COMPOSITION
by Ted Pease
Berklee College of Music legend Ted Pease demystifies the processes involved in writing jazz tunes and in composing episodic and extended jazz works.
50448000 Book/Online Audio $39.99

MODERN JAZZ VOICINGS
by Ted Pease and Ken Pullig
The definitive text used for the time-honored Chord Scales course at Berklee College of Music, this book concentrates on scoring for every possible ensemble combination.
50449485 Book/Online Audio $24.99

MUSIC COMPOSITION FOR FILM AND TELEVISION
by Lalo Schifrin
Learn film-scoring techniques from one of the great film/television composers of our time.
50449604 Book $34.99

MUSIC NOTATION
by Mark McGrain
Learn the essentials of music notation, from fundamental pitch and rhythm placement to intricate meter and voicing alignments.
50449399 .... $24.95

MUSIC NOTATION
by Matthew Nicholl and Richard Grudzinski
Whether you notate music by hand or use computer software, this practical reference will show you today's best practices rendering the details of your scores and parts.
50449540 Book $16.99

REHARMONIZATION TECHNIQUES
by Randy Felts
You'll find simple and innovative techniques to update songs and develop exciting new arrangements by studying the hundreds of copyrighted examples throughout this book.
50449496 Book $29.99

Berklee
Press

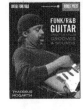
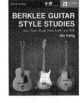

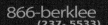